The Spanish Inquisition

MAJOR ISSUES IN HISTORY

Editor
C. WARREN HOLLISTER,
University of California, Santa Barbara

The Spanish Inquisition

EDITED BY

Paul J. Hauben
Department of History
University of The Pacific
Stockton, California

John Wiley & Sons, Inc.
New York   London   Sydney   Toronto

Library of Congress Catalogue Card Number: 71-91161

SBN 471 36000 7 (cloth)   SBN 471 36001 5 (paper)

Printed in the United States of America

For Janet, Rachel, John
and Karen

SERIES PREFACE

The reading program in a history survey course traditionally has consisted of a large two-volume textbook and, perhaps, a book of readings. This simple reading program requires few decisions and little imagination on the instructor's part, and tends to encourage in the student the virtue of careful memorization. Such programs are by no means things of the past, but they certainly do not represent the wave of the future.

The reading program in survey courses at many colleges and universities today is far more complex. At the risk of over-simplification, and allowing for many exceptions and overlaps, it can be divided into four categories: (1) textbook, (2) original source readings, (3) specialized historical essays and interpretive studies, and (4) historical problems.

After obtaining an overview of the course subject matter (textbook), sampling the original sources, and being exposed to selective examples of excellent modern historical writing (historical essays), the student can turn to the crucial task of weighing various possible interpretations of major historical issues. It is at this point that memory gives way to creative critical thought. The "problems approach," in other words, is the intellectual climax of a thoughtfully conceived reading program and is, indeed, the most characteristic of all approaches to historical pedagogy among the newer generation of college and university teachers.

The historical problems books currently available are many and varied. Why add to this information explosion? Because the Wiley Major Issues Series constitutes an endeavor to produce something new that will respond to pedagogical needs thus far unmet. First, it is a series of individual volumes—one per problem. Many good teachers would much prefer to select their own historical issues rather than be tied to an inflexible sequence of issues imposed by a publisher and bound together between two covers. Second, the Wiley Major Issues Series is based on the idea of approaching the significant problems of history through a deft interweaving of primary sources and secondary analysis, fused together by the skill of a scholar-editor. It is felt that the essence of a historical issue cannot be satisfactorily probed either by placing a body of undigested source materials into the hands of inexperienced students or by limiting these students to the controversial literature of modern scholars who debate the meaning of sources the student never sees. This series approaches historical problems by exposing students to both the finest historical thinking on the issue and some of the evidence on which this thinking is based. This synthetic approach should prove far more fruitful than either the raw-source approach or the exclusively second-hand approach, for it combines the advantages—and avoids the serious disadvantages—of both.

Finally, the editors of the individual volumes in the Major Issues Series have been chosen from among the ablest scholars in their fields. Rather than faceless referees, they are historians who know their issues from the inside and, in most instances, have themselves contributed significantly to the relevant scholarly literature. It has been the editorial policy of this series to permit the editor-scholars of the individual volumes the widest possible latitude both in formulating their topics and in organizing their materials. Their scholarly competence has been unquestioningly respected; they have been encouraged to approach the problems as they see fit. The titles and themes of the series volumes have been suggested in nearly every case by the scholar-editors themselves. The criteria have been (1) that the issue be of relevance to undergraduate lecture courses in history, and (2) that it be an issue which the scholar-editor knows thoroughly and in which he has done creative work. And, in general, the second criterion has been given precedence over the first. In short, the question "What are the significant historical issues today?" has been answered not by general editors or sales departments but by the scholar-teachers who are responsible for these volumes.

University of California,
Santa Barbara

C. Warren Hollister

ACKNOWLEDGMENTS

I am indebted to the following people for their constructive help in putting together my manuscript. First, I thank Professor C. Julian Bishko of the History Department of the University of Virginia. His incisive and detailed critique of the entire work was a model of that old, often-abused cliché, "constructive criticism." The introduction, in particular, was enhanced by his comments. I also thank Professor Albert A. Sicroff of the Romance Languages Department of Queens College, City University of New York, and Professor Haim Beinart of the Hebrew University of Jerusalem, who were also very helpful in their remarks regarding certain parts of the manuscript. Naturally, any faults that remain are mine.

I must pay a broader tribute to men and women throughout the academic world, working in areas of Hispanic studies. Their willingness to assist newcomers to the field is quite remarkable and, I suspect, regrettably unusual.

William Gum, the former senior editor at Wiley, and associate editor, Nancy Unger Lipscomb, deserve warm thanks for getting this project under way. Barry Benjamin put the arduous editorial finishing touches through final production. My typist, Mrs. Andi Rains, did a superb job in record time. My wife, Janet Hauben, showed her customary patience toward her husband, who is not always a model of patience and fortitude during a research and writing process.

PAUL J. HAUBEN

CONTENTS

NOTES ON THE CONTRIBUTORS

JOHN H. ELLIOTT holds the chair of History at King's College, University of London. He also has authored the *Revolt of the Catalans* (Cambridge University Press, 1963).

JOHN LYNCH, Lecturer in Hispanic and Latin American History at University College, London, has also published in colonial Latin American history, and is at work on vol. II of *Spain under the Habsburgs (1598-1700)*.

MIGUEL DE LA PINTA LLORENTE is a Spanish cleric and church historian with a special interest in the Inquisition. He has also written several more specialized studies revolving about notable inquisitorial trials in the sixteenth century, none available in English unfortunately; the most recent proves the Judaic-converso lineage of J. L. Vives, the great early 16th century Spanish humanist and close friend of Erasmus.

JUAN ANTONIO LLORENTE (1756-1823) was a secretary for the Inquisition who turned against it and used his office to gather data for his anticlerical tract, here excerpted from. He became a follower of the French satellite government under Napoleon's brother, Joseph. For all of its obvious biases, Llorente's work was the first with any serious documentation.

HENRY CHARLES LEA was the great American historian around 1900 who provided students with the first really scholarly study of the Inquisition, upon which all others have leaned. The fame and availability of this work, and the difficulty of excerpting from its very minutely detailed pages, led me to use only the brief but representative notice from it. Among Lea's other books were *Chapters from the Religious History of Spain, A History of the Inquisition in the Middle Ages, A History of the Spanish Inquisition in the Dependencies*.

Notes on the Contributors

R. TREVOR DAVIES, who died in 1953, was Lecturer in Spanish History at Oxford University. He also wrote *Spain in Decline, 1621–1700* (reissued in paper ed., London–New York, 1965).

HENRY KAMEN, Lecturer in History at the University of Warwick, has just added *The Rise of Toleration* (New York, 1967, paper ed.) to his publications. He also translates Russian poetry.

BEN-ZION NETANYAHU of Dropsie College, Philadelphia, Pennsylvania, is working on a new history of the Spanish Inquisition.

FRANCISCO MÁRQUEZ VILLANUEVA, author of several significant monographs on the conversos in the fifteenth century, especially in Castile, was at Harvard University during 1964–1965.

SIR CECIL ROTH is an internationally-known Anglo-Jewish student of Jewish history, particularly of the Sephardic Mediterranean communities.

YTZHAK FRITZ BAER, Professor Emeritus of the Hebrew University of Jerusalem, Israel, was born and trained in Germany. One of his works, a general two-volume history of the Jews in Spain, is in English. He has trained a great number of current Jewish and Israeli historians and is intimately involved in many ongoing professional endeavors and organizations.

ERNST SCHÄFER also authored, in Spanish, the standard work on the Council of the Indies in 1935.

JOHN E. LONGHURST, Professor of History at the University of Kansas, has written numerous articles and monographs on early sixteenth century Spanish heterodoxy.

R. GONSALVIUS MONTANUS (Gonzalez Montes) was a pseudonym for one or more unknown and probably Spanish Protestant exiles. This work went through several editions in several languages through the early seventeenth century and greatly helped to shape Protestant views of Spain for many years.

The Spanish Inquisition

INTRODUCTION

The Spanish Inquisition has been called many things, from the resolute defender of Catholicism to the earliest version of the Nazi Gestapo. Its history is often confounded with racialism, religious tyranny, obnoxious legal procedures, the permanent delaying of Spanish modernization, and other equally regressive matters. For these reasons I have selected readings that exemplify the historiography of this subject, as well as those that describe its workings. Indeed, to this day, the attitudes toward the Inquisition, or Holy Office as it was also named, among professional historians as well as laymen, are frequently an index of broadly liberal or conservative approaches to present-day issues affecting Spain and, often, the world in general. Similarly, specialized and popular interpretations of such great events as the American Civil War usually cast a long shadow on the present. The Spanish Inquisition—indeed, what to make of Spain's great imperial past, of which the Holy Office was so significant a part—remains a burning coal in the national conscience and consciousness. In its own way it is as emotional a term as perhaps "free enterprise" is for many Americans, "liberty, fraternity, and equality" for the French, and the "dictatorship of the proletariat" for Communists the world over.

Precisely why is the study of this institution not merely an antiquarian endeavor? In large part, I think, it is because the Inquisition's history so closely paralleled the time of national greatness, although it continued to function well beyond the mid-seventeenth century, the approximate terminal date to Spanish hegemony. Many of the tribunal's defenders, while often regretting its excesses as they saw them, still interpreted its role as a necessary constituent of that lost national supremacy in Europe and much of the world from about 1500-1650. Others suggest that the Inquisition, instead, sapped Spanish internal

strength by destroying much of the more productive and
energetic elements of society; Spain maintained her greatness
despite this corrosive oppression, and the Holy Office, in the last
analysis, helped lead to, if it was not in fact the primary cause
of, the national decline, a subject of considerable—and often
nostalgic—fascination to Spaniards and scholars alike. Still others,
regardless of this broadly imperial issue, regard the Inquisition
as having been absolutely mandatory for true national unification, achieved under Ferdinand and Isabella, who also established
this tribunal in the late fifteenth century. In this sense, perhaps,
subsequent results, even unfortunate ones, are not really central
to the discussion. The rebuttal here suggests that this state-
founded ecclesiastical organ came to usurp secular authority.
Varieties of these views will be found in the selections.

Historians and laymen alike are fascinated by the origins of
an institution, a nation, a religion. For students of the Spanish
Inquisition, this question is of crucial significance: Why was
Christian Spain after about 1350 unable to continue the medieval
tradition of religious pluralism in both the Moslem and Christian
parts of the Iberian peninsula? Why was a separate Holy Office
instituted in Castile in 1478 and shortly thereafter extended by
the Crown to the three states of the Kingdom of Aragon
(Catalonia, Valencia, and Aragon, with the Balearic Isles) at a
time when the medieval, nonnational Papal Inquisition had
become virtually moribund? Some recapitulation of the preceding years is necessary.

Fundamental to a comprehension of Spanish history is the
realization of the impact of the seven-centuries long reconquest
of the peninsula from the Moors; legendarily, what was lost in
seven years took as many arduous (and interrupted) centuries of
effort to regain. From the regional and sometimes chronologi-
cally dissimilar nature of this vast military crusade came political
fragmentation, which ultimately crystallized in the steadily
larger Christian crowns of Portugal, Castile, and Aragon, with
the last, as noted above, consisting of three distinct states in a
dynastic union. In both Moorish and Christian territories Jewish
minorities existed, occasionally subjected to explosions of religious intolerance, but until about the third quarter of the fourteenth century living in comparative tranquillity, especially

when contrasted with the lot of other European Jewish popula-
tions. Most Jews were urban and were significant or even
dominant, in some cases, in many of the professions such as
medicine and law. Many were prominent in royal, municipal,
and seignorial administration as estate managers, tax collectors,
and the like, while the mass of lesser Jews figured importantly
in the artisan crafts. To a considerable extent, particularly in times
of social and political stress, the fact that so many Jews were intimately involved in high office and finance, served merely to
accentuate their always potentially exposed situation in Spanish
life. In brief, by the mid-fourteenth century, because of their
very success in what we can loosely designate as upper middle-
class functions, the Spanish Jewish community had unwittingly
positioned itself to be the scapegoat for "bad times."

In conjunction with the rest of western and central Europe,
Spain underwent a series of enormous shocks, commencing with
the great epidemic of the Black Death (bubonic plague) of
1348-1351, which struck a continent already caught up in socioeconomic difficulties and endemic warfare. Not until the last
third of the following century did Europe begin generally to
emerge from the vicious and, to contemporaries, inexplicable
cycle of epidemics, civil and international wars of great destruction, continued economic dislocation, political chaos, and religious crises, such as the Great Schism (1378-1415), which
rent Christendom into hostile papacies. To many, the sole explanation for this general collapse of Western Christianity from
the medieval heights of the twelfth and thirteenth centuries was
to interpret the array of seemingly connected calamities as God's
will and just scourge.[1]

For long stretches of this period both Castile and Aragon
were characterized by royal children occupying the thrones
(who too often grew to become ineffectual adult rulers), great
rural and urban discontent, occasional breakdowns of law and
order, and the like; all these occurring in the generally retrograde conditions described above. (It must be noted that Cata-

[1] Ingamar Bergman's great film, *The Seventh Seal*, set in Sweden in the
1370's, admirably catches the extreme reactions to these disasters. See also
J. Huizinga's masterly study, *The Waning of the Middle Ages* (New York,
1956).

lonia suffered most in terms of population decline, the ferocity
of domestic strife, etc.; recent research has indicated the basic
health of the Castilian economy by comparison, although most
Castilians at the time saw matters otherwise.)

It is not surprising, then, that many people, clerical and lay,
saw in the seemingly paramount role of the Jews the chief
reason for God's anger and Castile-Aragon's tribulations. By
this time, too, the Moors had been reduced in territorial control
to the southern strip of Castile around Granada, while the many
Moors in Christian lands were petty artisans and peasants, who
had not meaningfully infiltrated the more important occupations,
as the Jews had. Under the grave strains of the later middle
ages, the earlier tolerance evaporated, and the anti-Jewish po-
groms of 1391, starting at Seville, rapidly spread across the
cities and small towns of Castile and Aragon, whipped on by the
fiery anti-Semitic sermons of members of the mendicant (begging) orders, the Franciscans and Dominicans. This crusade of
the lower clergy and lay poor, often with upper-class assistance
or connivance, curiously foreshadowed in large part the great
guerrilla war against the Napoleonic occupation some four centuries later. It is to be noted, however, that the rulers and large
segments of the nobility and municipal oligarchies attempted,
usually with little or no success, to protect local Jews, out of
recognition of their vital roles in the economy and administration. Indeed, unlike the rest of western Europe where Christians
had long ousted Jews from broadly similar commercial positions,
the Spanish Christians, not without exceptions to be sure, had
remained peasants, men of arms, and clergy. The Reconquest
had firmly implanted its military-religious-landowning values of
the permanent crusade, particularly in the Castilian heartland,
where it took longest. Manual labor and "bourgeois" values and
activities were largely looked down upon.

Nonetheless, there was no disputing the need for the middle
class and hitherto largely non-Christian doctors, financiers, ad-
ministrators, and the like. In this regard the very course of the
1391 riots provided a short-run partial solution. This was not
genocide or enforced departure, but mass conversion under pressure which, however, was incomplete. The Christian kings and

protectors of the Jews could hardly repudiate conversions once
(and for all) accomplished, regardless of their circumstances.
Thus the creation of the New Christians, or conversos and
marranos[2] as they were alternately called, ensued with tremen-
dously important immediate and eventual consequences. Until
about 1420, local pressures caused a fairly steady increase among
the converts both in Aragon and Castile; then, temporarily, the
external stimuli to conversion slackened, as moments of religious
fanaticism or repression frequently do when they are not
institutionalized. Along with the remaining Jews, most of whose
communities *(aljamas, juderías)* survived in the smaller towns
where, apparently, they had been more artisans than members of
the administrative-financial elite, the New Christians simply
resumed their previously vital functions, especially in the
Aragonese states where they fully supplanted practicing Jews
in these areas.

Among Jews in and out of Spain in the extent of the conversions, both forced and voluntary, in the largest and most pros-
perous of European Jewish communities and among the religious
and secular elite of that community, created great distress and
bewilderment as explanations were sought. To a considerable
degree, then and now, the secularizing tendencies of medieval
philosophy, loosely grouped under "Averroism,"[3] which had
eroded the essentials of Judaism precisely among its educated
elite, were blamed; others, like Christians, saw in these defections
God's wrath against His people for their transgressions. These
opinions notwithstanding, there remained large numbers of converts who secretly practiced Judaism entirely or in part throughout these years. The readings abundantly point out all the

[2] Marrano originally was a very insulting word of Moslem derivation,
meaning pig.

[3] "Averroism," a radical form of medieval Aristotelianism, denied, among
other things, immortality as Christians and Jews understood it. By this time,
among Spanish Jews, it had come also to embrace a religious skepticism,
inasmuch as no faith was thought worth suffering for; individual philosophic
realization came first. John Calvin would have labelled its adherents "Lib-
ertines" and "Nicodemites." Still, many Jewish Averroists became devout
and even anti-Semitic Catholics.

options for Jews and converts alike under these strained conditions.

By the middle of the fifteenth century, then, the New Christians had become as feared and despised by the run of the Spanish people as the Jews had been (and still were) in previous generations, and for the same reasons. To those was added religio-racial distrust: increasingly the conversos' sincerity became suspect. The depth of this feeling was to mean, in this regard, that the upturn in the general fortunes of the Iberian states, culminating in the unification of Castile and Aragon by the marriage and achievements of Ferdinand of Aragon and Isabella of Castile, would be largely irrelevant in this issue of faith. The Spanish people never overcame their basic religious insecurity, a product primarily of the trauma of the fourteenth and fifteenth centuries. The Old Christian (as "pure" Spanish Christians came to be called from this time) reaction took two related forms: the *limpieza de sangre* statutes, which insisted that a candidate for a particular ecclesiastical or secular post prove his Christian ancestry, beginning at Toledo, where a large, prominent converso community flourished, in 1449; and the establishment of the Holy Office almost three decades later. It would be redundant, with respect to the readings, to discuss the Inquisition further at this point; I leave general and final considerations to my prefaces to each selection and to the conclusion. Suffice it to say here that the purity of blood decrees could be sidestepped by falsified, often expensive genealogies, usually obtained by the wealthy and the noble—the very ones who often successfully avoided the inquisitors—but there is no doubt that these statutes reflected popular pressures and contributed to that air of religious, social, and psychological unease to which I shall return in the conclusion.

By 1492 the rulers of united Spain, fresh from the eradication of the last independent Islamic state in the peninsula, were persuaded that inquisitorial testing of the conversos' religious sincerity was insufficient; the congregations of practicing Jews had to go in order to avert the temptation to return to the ancient faith. Indeed, it was commonly believed that reconversion was increasing, abetted by zealous Jews—hence, the expulsion. Nonetheless, Judaizing,[4] the clandestine observance of various Jewish practices continued to keep the Inquisition busy, with the assistance of informing on a fairly large scale.

In this drive for religious unity and conformity, it is essential to remark that Spain was hardly unique. Jews had been expelled from other countries in the middle ages, and Catholic and Protestant lands alike were characterized by similar beliefs on the necessity of religious uniformity shortly thereafter. But in these other regions the Jews had not achieved so significant and enduring a socioeconomic niche, nor were large numbers of suspect converts forcibly (by and large) created. As we have seen, the latter were both indispensable and hated: the blood statutes and the Inquisition resulted to institutionalize the drive for religious conformity in a unique and successful way. These events coincided with the unfolding of national, particularly Castilian greatness; hence, the profound cultural, intellectual, and religious problem, centering on the Inquisition, posed then and now to students of the Hispanic reality.

During the 1520's and 1530's, the Spanish Inquisition acquired new grounds for its investigation which, however, were intimately related to its original jurisdictional reason for being, the scrutiny of the conversos' religious sincerity. Illuminism—a peculiarly Castilian form of mysticism, the most interior kind of religious experience—emerged in the first third of the sixteenth century with particular intensity among devout clergy and laymen (and women, who figured with unusual prominence, foreshadowing a St. Teresa in more ways than sex) of frequently New Christian background. The end of the fifteenth century and first decades of the new one—the classic pre-Reformation period—were marked in Castile by much religious reform and striving, not unlike Europe as a whole. Under the auspices of the Catholic Kings, as Ferdinand and Isabella were named during their joint reign, Cardinal Ximenez de Cisneros,

[4] Spain's annexation of Portugal in 1580 caused the influx of numerous descendents of Spanish Jews who fled there, only to give in to conversion pressures there after 1496 in response to Spanish pressures on Portugal. Attracted by new opportunities in Castile, they sharply increased the Judaizing problem again.

former Franciscan and confessor to the Queen, not only was
Grand Inquisitor, *de facto* first minister of the state, and successful advocate of punitive measures against recalcitrant Granadan
Moors after the 1492 conquest, but also patronized the founding
of the University of Alcala, dedicated in large part to the
education of an effective episcopate and religious scholarship,
the partly successful reform of the mendicant orders, and the
intrusion of Erasmism.

The post-1391 situation had seen many Jewish religious and
intellectual leaders become influential members of the Roman
Catholic ecclesiastical hierarchy, some of whom, as noted, led
the continuing assault on their former faith. But the illuminists
(alumbrados) in their often excessive disregard for Catholicism's externals, its ceremonies and rituals, even its sacraments,
seemed dangerously near heresy. That so many were of doubt-
ful religious lineage clearly helped to arouse the Holy Office's
suspicions, and its jurisdiction in such cases was clear enough.
This distrust of the differently intense character of these pious
conversos' faith manifested itself in a series of investigations,
trials, and outcomes of often adverse nature that continued on
through the days of St. Teresa and Luis de Leon half a century
later.

Coincidental with and intertwined with Illuminism in many
individuals was the rise of Castilian Erasmianism. Erasmus, sometimes too superficially compared to Voltaire, combined the
methodology of Italian Humanism with a genuine Christian
faith. Through his writings he had become, on the eve of the
Reformation, the acknowleged champion of Christian Humanism; indeed, it is perhaps not farfetched to suggest that he did,
less systematically of course, for Humanism what Aquinas had
done for the more clearly non-Christian Aristotelianism of the
thirteenth century. The accession of the Flemish-bred
Emperor Charles V to the Spanish throne through an incredible
series of dynastic marriages, births, and deaths[5] accelerated the

[5] Eldest son of the Catholic Kings' sole surviving child, Joanna, and the
Emperor Maximilian I's only son, Philip (died 1506). King Charles I of
Spain, 1516–1556, became Emperor following Maximilian I's death in 1519.
His international court was for a time permeated with seemingly Erasmian
courtiers and secretaries.

Castilian stimuli to the spread of Erasmianism in a tight coterie of courtiers, academics, and some clergy. Erasmianism called for the renewal of a Christian life along basically moral-ethical lines. In its call for an educated, well-motivated clergy and purified religious scholarship, it obtained the support of Cardinal Cisneros and other influential Castilians, religious and lay. In its rejection of medieval scholasticism and often violent diatribes against clerical, especially monastic abuses, it soon earned the enmity of the Dominicans in particular, who staffed the Inquisition and, not surprisingly, generally upheld Thomism. Indeed, in its use of humanist techniques in scriptural scholarship, the conservatives noted with distress and anger that at certain key points doctrine seemed to be sacrificed for linguistic purity. Erasmus' own 1516 Greek New Testament aroused a furor in this regard in its handling of the Trinity, for instance. More congenial to the leaders of Spain was that part of the Erasmian program calling for the reform of Christendom through the secular monarchs (in cooperation with the Papacy, however), since the Church seemed unable to reform itself. In this respect, much of the Spanish clergy agreed; it resembled the French Catholic Church in its resentment of papal interference, and both tended to be royalist. Last but not least, and from the Inquisition's viewpoint too much like the suspect Illuminists, in practice Erasmians, many of whom also were of converso background, seemed to rather take for granted church externals and to concentrate more on the interior matters of faith. At no time, however, did Erasmus and his followers, especially those in Spain, consider themselves anything but devout Catholics and, subsequently, many of their suggestions, such as the renewal of effective preaching, were taken up by Catholics and Protestants. These developments, however, failed to save Spanish Erasmianism from its particular debacle, while the movement generally fell afoul of new religious intransigency as the century progressed toward permanent Christian schism and religious war.

The outbreak of Protestantism, with its apparent similarities to Spanish Erasmianism and Illuminism in the eyes of many Spaniards, not just inquisitors, permitted the latter to tie the two firmly together and brand them as expressions of "Lutheranism." Was not the northern heresy religiously subjective and individ-

ualistic? antisacramental and anticeremonial? doctrinally un-
Christian? The tactic of combining Erasmianism, Illuminism, and
Lutheranism into one convenient "heretical package"[6] worked
very well, assisted by the withdrawal of royal support for
Erasmianism for basically extrareligious reasons after 1529.[7] By
about 1540 Spanish Erasmianism was dead, if one can indeed
designate it as a serious movement; certainly it always lacked
organized or institutional backing, and was overly dependent on
the favor of a handful of well-placed but not overmighty persons. Nonetheless, its "underground" influence continued later
in this century in the revival of biblical studies under Philip II.
Illuminism, more diffused in a grass-roots sense among clergy
and devout laity, and not, like Erasmianism, confined to more
visible groups and hence more exposed to successful attack,
contributed to the great flowering of Spanish mysticism culminating in the figures of St. Teresa, St. John of the Cross, and
others. To be sure, even these saints occasionally ran afoul of
inquisitorial suspicions on Illuminist grounds.

The reaction to the exposure of two seemingly Protestant
conventicles in 1558 at Valladolid and Seville, with the involve-
ment of many New Christians in them, gave the Inquisition a
new impetus in mid-century, and a solid role in the most recent
of Spanish crusades against Protestantism, increasingly viewed
as an international menace to nation and faith. The relative
fewness of the native Protestants and the general ferocity of
the national response to their uncovering reveals the totally un-
statistical quality of Spanish thought concerning heresy. In this
attitude Spain was not unique; rather, she expressed it with
perhaps greater intensity, accompanied by institutional possibilities of acting it out, worked out earlier against her native non-
Christian and superficially Christian subjects. Clearly, by the
middle of the Reformation century Protestantism was to Spain

---

[6] J. E. Longhurst's remark. Note in the Elliott selection the futile effort
by the Erasmian head of the Inquisition in 1525 to detach Erasmianism from
Illuminism by condemning the latter; the inquisitorial rank and file literally
passively and successfully resisted him.

[7] Charles' accord with the Pope and his ensuing several years' absence
from Spain undercut Erasmianism and the Inquisition mounted its final successful assault on it at this time.

what Communism was to America around 1950, the diminutive
number of American Communists notwithstanding. Equally as
clearly, the significance of the Spanish Protestant episode lay
in its internal consequences, and the enormous impetus it gave
to a growingly dark view of Spain abroad, even in other Catholic countries, in conjunction with other factors. It is rather
ironic that it was the harsh treatment of the handful of indigen-
ous Protestants that helped create the international image of the
Spain of the "Black Legend," not the more lasting grinding
down of thousands of Jews, conversos, and others. Doubly
ironic is the probability that a substantial number of these
presumed Protestants, if not the majority, were more likely
latter-day Erasmians or "liberal" Catholics rather than "Lutherans" as such. But one scarcely could have expected otherwise:
the Reformation would be concerned only with its own.

I have so far discussed those areas central to the selections.
Since the Jewish-converso issue was fundamental to the Inquisition's establishment, and the Erasmian-Illuminist-Protestant issue
was fundamental to both the institutional and national situation and reputation for a long time, I concentrated on them. The
Morisco problem (Moors nominally Christianized) and the
matter of witchcraft, while of considerable interest to the Holy
Office, do not, I feel, merit such attention. One of the readings
briefly touches on the latter in passing; as has been recently
suggested, correctly in my view, sorcery and allied issues was a
pan-European problem at this time. In fact, it has long been
commonplace to remark upon Spain's comparative freedom from
most of Europe's witchcraft mania from the late middle ages to
the seventeenth century, which coincided with the Inquisition's
height of power. This entire topic lies outside our scope; I
refer the interested student to the bibliography following the
conclusion.

Demographically, the Moriscos were a fairly substantial group,
important in the Castilian silk industry and the specialized, ir-
rigated farming of Valencia and the Ebro valley in Aragon.
With threatening Mohammedan states, headed by the formid-
able Ottoman Empire, ringing the Mediterranean, Spaniards always felt uneasy about the superficially Christianized population
of Islamic origin and way of life in their midst. This insecurity

contributed solidly to the Moriscos' final expulsion in 1609. But despite the Spaniards' recurrent fear of Morisco collusion with the Ottoman and North African states of Islam, and several rebellions, one major (1568–1570), I am persuaded that they never constituted quite the threat the Jews and New Christians were felt to be. The Moriscos consciously and successfully refused to assimilate, and their occupations generally remained at the lower end of the economic scale; nominal Christianization altered their way of life far less than conversion seems to have done for the Jews. Although there was lower-class resentment from Old Christians against Morisco artisans, farmers, etc., and also fear of their tendency to reproduce at a faster rate, we hear of no great Morisco financiers, bureaucrats, clergy, and so forth. They simply were not a significant internal threat to Spanish society; they were not truly the enemy within the gates as the conversos clearly were looked upon, and so they are not central to our story.

I wish to conclude this introduction with a brief bibliographical note. There are three authors of great significance to this subject from whose works I have not excerpted, with the exception of one and very briefly. They are Américo Castro (1885–   ), who virtually began the sophisticated study of the impact of Jews and converts on Spanish culture, Marcelino Menéndez y Pelayo (1885–1912), whose massive defense of the Inquisition in the 1880's remains the keystone of the traditionalist approach, and Henry Charles Lea (1825–1909), the great American historian, whose monumental study of the Holy Office in the 1890's retains consistently scholarly value today. Their views are essentially reflected in the readings, the second part of which made it unnecessary to use Lea's voluminous documentary compilations, which incidentally are still in print and readily available. Lea, in fact, overcame the bias of his age suggested in his introductory statement to his great work, noted in Part I. Castro, it should be observed, considers the Inquisition's reason for being, attitudes, and procedures, a mirror image of the clannishness and sense of religious superiority of the Spanish Jewish communities themselves; here, he seems to have overtaxed his evidence, as Jewish scholars especially have been quick to note. Finally, as I state below, the conservative interpretation of Menéndez y Pelayo is well represented in the passages chosen from the recent work of Miguel de la Pinta Llorente. Last but assuredly not least, I have relied quite heavily upon Y. F. Baer's general history of the Jews in Christian Spain, especially the second volume. The student is referred to the bibliography for specific citations.

PART ONE

Historiographical and Descriptive

In Part One of the readings I have attempted to give the reader a brief, clear description of the workings and structure of the Inquisition (Lynch and Elliott), and at greater length, an idea of the varying ways in which the study of the institution has been undertaken. Very quickly, it becomes obvious that the Spanish Inquisition has been the touchstone for emotionally conflicting interpretations, whose implications often go well beyond the confines of aspects of the Holy Office itself. As sections of Part II demonstrate, this is by no means a modern problem only.

1   John Lynch and John Elliott
Recent Scholarly and Secular Views

John Elliott and John Lynch are two contemporary English historians of early modern Spain who have on the whole successfully freed themselves from both the classically traditional views of Anglo-Saxon, Protestant, liberal contempt and moralizing over the Inquisition and the defensively polemicizing attitude toward it, which marks the Pinta Llorente selections and which, as those from the slightly earlier Englishman, Trevor Davies, will show, was not confined to Spaniards alone. Indeed, the comparison between the two more recent

15

*English scholars and their immediate Oxford predecessor virtually
sums up the enormous differences between careful historians and
those students of a subject whose main commitment is to its apology
and defense, rather than its analysis and comprehension. Thus the
study of the Spanish Inquisition and, by extension, of the problem
of the "decline of Spain," is of a nature similar to the study of the
French Revolution, and American and English Civil Wars, where
passions similarly engaged often obscure scholarship. In this sense at
least, Elliott and Lynch have cleared the air regarding early modern
Spain as a whole.*

Elliott, p. 96. "It may therefore have been influential *conversos*
at court and in the ecclesiastical hierarchy who first pressed for
the establishment of the Inquisition in Castile . . ." [because
they] "were afraid that their own position would be jeopar-
dized by the backsliding of their brethren." (This statement
essentially sums up the Américo Castro[1] line of reasoning regarding the founding of the tribunal. Ed.) Cf. Lynch, p. 21.
"Finally, many of the New Christians became the bitterest
enemies of their former brethren. Anxious to protest their own
orthodoxy and to protect themselves against the suspicions of
the Old Christians, converts denounced not only Jews but also
fellow converts, and this spirit of rivalry and jealousy may have
aggravated the intolerance of the Inquisition itself; many officials
of the early Spanish Inquisition, including Torquemada, were
descended from New Christians." [This is still arguable specifically regarding Torquemada, the Holy Office's first famous head.
Ed.] Page 21, note no. 21. "Américo Castro, *The Structure of
Spanish History*, trans. E. L. King (Princeton University Press,

[1] See Introduction for extended comments on his work.

SOURCES. John Elliott, *Imperial Spain, 1469–1716* (New York: St. Martin's
Press, 1964), pp. 96–97, 209, and 213. Reprinted by permission of St. Martin's
Press, New American Library, Inc., Edward Arnold (Publishers) Ltd. and
the author. John Lynch, *Spain Under The Hapsburgs, 1516–1598*, Vol. 1
(Oxford: Basil Blackwell, 1964), pp. 21, 33, and 26. Reprinted by permis-
sion of the publisher and the author.

1954), pp. 421-430, 532, 540 argues that 'the Inquisition had been in the making since the beginning of the fifteenth century,' largely by 'deserters from Israel.' The thesis is not entirely convincing."

Elliott, p. 97, on motives behind the Inquisition's establishment by Ferdinand and Isabella, the Catholic Kings, especially concerning the traditional stress on political and administrative aspects: "The imposition of the new-style Inquisition in . . . Aragon as well as Castile [The crowns of Aragon—Aragon, Catalonia, and Valencia—had had a papal tribunal in the late middle ages regarding the Albigensians, etc.] is often regarded as a move by Ferdinand to increase his political control over his Aragonese possessions. . . . The Inquisition was the first institution, apart from the monarchy itself, common to the possessions of Spain, and it did . . . serve as a unifying organ. But it has yet to be proved that Ferdinand saw it as a weapon for destroying local autonomy and furthering . . . centralization. The conventional emphasis on Isabella's piety makes it easy to overlook [his] strong religious strain . . . a fervent devotee of the Virgin, an ardent supporter of ecclesiastical reform in Catalonia, and a man whose messianic brand of religion gave him many of the attributes of the *converso*. . . ."

Lynch, pp. 23-26. A basic structural and procedural description:

"The Spanish Inquisition was created in the form of a council of state, the Council of the Supreme and General Inquisition—usually called the Suprema—with jurisdiction in all matters of heresy. Thus the conciliar formula favoured by the Catholic Monarchs for the solution of their administrative problems was applied to religion too. To secure royal control over the new institution and exclude that of the pope, the monarchs then had to ensure that the president of the Suprema had full control of the appointment and dismissal of individual inquisitors, and that they themselves controlled the president. Therefore they created a new office, unknown to the medieval Inquisition, an Inquisitor General, who presided over the meetings of the Suprema and was head of the entire Inquisition. Appointment to the office of Inquisitor General rested exclusively with the crown, as did appointment of subordinate officials, though in practice these

were usually appointed by the Inquisitor General and the
Suprema. In this way the crown avoided both the possibility
of papal intervention and the danger of the Inquisition itself
becoming independent. The Suprema, also appointed by the
crown, consisted of six members, who included representatives
of the Dominican order and the Council of Castile. It heard
appeals form the local tribunals, and also controlled the financial
administration of the Inquisition, its property and the proceeds
of its confiscations, the profits of which went to the royal
treasury.

"Canonically, as the Inquisition was an ecclesiastical tribunal,
the pope was its head. In theory this was admitted by the
Spanish authorities, but in practice papal jurisdiction was rigidly
excluded. Similarly the papacy managed to cling to the princi-
ple of its appellate jurisdiction, but was unable to apply it. The
practical effect of this was that it became impossible to appeal a
case from the Spanish Inquisition to Rome, and in this direction
Spain was to set an example even to Protestant countries. In
matters of heresy the Inquisition had jurisdiction over all laymen
and clergy—but not bishops—to the exclusion of all other courts.
From its judgment there was no appeal, not even to the pope,
who in three centuries of the Spanish tribunal's existence managed to claim from it only three cases for his judgment. Independent of the papacy, the Spanish Inquisition was a close and
subordinate ally of the crown, and on more than one occasion its
authority was to be abused for political purposes. Indeed, this
dual character of the Spanish Inquisition, deriving from the
close alliance of church and state in Spain, was one of its most
peculiar features; it combined the spiritual authority of the
church with the temporal power of the crown.

"Operating under the central council of the Inquisition were
permanent local tribunals which represented for the mass of the
people the real embodiment of its power. There were some
thirteen of these tribunals in Spain, situated in the principal
towns; outside Spain tribunals operated in the Canaries, Sicily,
and Sardinia, and from the 1570's in the Indies. In each of these
tribunals there were two or three inquisitor-judges, a prosecuting attorney, various secretaries, together with *calificadores*, or
theological consultants; there were also minor officials such as

doctors and gaolers. The senior officials were usually chosen from the regular clergy—though they could be laymen. Attached to each tribunal, however, were a number of part-time agents called *familiares*, many of whom were laymen. Their identity was not always public knowledge and they were used for various duties ranging from spying to providing armed escorts for prisoners. The *familiares* formed a kind of police force at the disposal of the Inquisition, and although they were unpaid they enjoyed various perquisites and advantages which made them a privileged class with a vested interest in the Inquisition.

"The legal procedure of the Spanish Inquisition was marked by the fact that the tribunals combined two functions, judicial and police. They were not ordinary courts of law, because they also had powers of investigation, and in addition to the punishment of offenders they also wanted their confession and renunciation in order to save their souls. This dual purpose was reflected in the actual procedure they used. The procedure of the medieval Inquisition was by pure *inquisitio*, that is to say the inquisitor acted as both prosecutor and judge. Superficially the Spanish Inquisition proceeded more impartially, by way of *accusatio*, with a public prosecutor as an accuser and the inquisitors acting only as judges. But this was legal fiction and simply meant that the inquisitor had the assistance of a trained lawyer in making the prosecution; it was the inquisitors who gathered evidence, and like their medieval predecessors they were prosecutors as well as judges.

"Each locality had to be visited every year by an inquisitor who solemnly published an *Edict of Faith*, which, in the form of a minute questionnaire, imposed on every Christian under pain of major excommunication the obligation to denounce known heretics. When the tribunal itself saw a suspicious situation—which was mainly in the first century of its existence—it would begin by publishing an *Edict of Grace*, which allowed a period of 30-40 days to all who wished to come forward voluntarily to confess faults and errors. Confession usually meant pardon and only light penalties, but there was a condition attached—that the penitent reveal his accomplices. Both edicts were open to serious abuses. In particular, the Edict of Faith, by enjoining denunciations, forced the faithful to co-operate in the work of the Inquisition and made everyone its agent or its spy, offering moreover an irresistible temptation for the relief of private malice. The two edicts usually led to a crop of denunciations—which were also expected to contain the names of witnesses—and it was either these or the investigations of the inquisitors themselves which initiated the legal proceedings.

"If the accusations were accepted then the accused was imprisoned in the secret gaols of the Inquisition, usually in humane conditions, but utterly secluded from the outside world and deprived of all contact with his family and friends. The case then proceeded, slowly and in strict secrecy, and based throughout on the assumption that the accused was guilty. But the greatest defect in the legal procedure of the Spanish Inquisition was the fact that the accused was kept uninformed about the identity of his accusers and their witnesses, who were thereby relieved from responsibility, while the accused was left largely helpless in preparing his defence. His only safeguard was that he could draw up a list of his enemies, and if it contained any of the accusers then their evidence would be discounted. Otherwise almost any kind of evidence and any type of witness were accepted for the prosecution, whereas the questions put to the defense witnesses, and whether they were called at all, were entirely at the discretion of the inquisitors. Once the case for the prosecution was ready, the organization of the defense could begin. The accused was allowed an officially appointed lawyer, but he could refuse him and request another. He was also provided with a counsellor whose function it was to convince him that he should make a sincere confession. The pressure of the counsellor, together with the secrecy of the accusers and witnesses, undoubtedly weakened the position of the defendant which his own lawyer and witnesses could hardly be expected to redress. Indeed, the secrecy of informers and witnesses was an innovation in Spain, alarming to contemporaries, and contrary to the procedure of other courts of law. But the situation of the accused was rendered even more desperate by the power of the Inquisition, like other tribunals of the time, to use torture to procure evidence and confession. Bloodshed and anything likely to cause permanent injury were forbidden, but this still left room for three painful methods of torture, all of which were well known and not peculiar to the Inquisition: the rack, the hoist, and the water torture. Even if their use was infrequent and accompanied by medical safeguards, they were horribly inappropriate in matters of conscience.

"After evidence had been taken and qualified theologians consulted if necessary—all of which invariably took a long time, sometimes four or five years—sentence was passed. If the accused confessed his guilt in the course of the trial *before* sentence was passed and his confession was accepted, then he was absolved and dismissed with lighter punishment. Otherwise sentence would be acquittal or condemnation. A verdict of guilty did not necessarily mean death. It depended first of all on the gravity of the offence, and the penalties, which were derived from medieval civil and canon law, might involve penance, fine or flogging for minor offences, and the dreaded galleys or crippling confiscation of property for more serious ones. But it also depended on many other factors, such as the circumstances of the times, the character of the accused, and above all on the temperament of the judges, not all of whom were equally relentless. In proportion to the number of cases the death penalty was rare. On the other hand a repentant heretic who relapsed again never escaped the death penalty. Those who persisted in heresy, or in their denial of guilt, were burnt alive. Those who repented at the last minute and *after* sentence, whether sincerely or not, were strangled first, then burnt. The execution itself was not performed by the Inquisition but by the civil authorities. The Spanish *auto de fe* was merely an elaborately staged public exhibition at which the sentence was pronounced and discussed amidst much ceremony. The heretic was then 'relaxed' to the secular arm, which carried out the sentence of burning, often at a different time and place. Beginning as a means of instilling awe and terror in the faithful, the *auto de fe* soon degenerated into a social occasion of perverse excitement and became a kind of religious entertainment to celebrate a royal wedding or a monarch's visit or some other public function. But only major cases were completed with an *auto de fe*. In minor ones the sentences were published privately."

Elliott, pp. 209-213. The assault on Erasmism and further reflections:

"In 1527 Archbishop Manrique, hoping to draw the sting of Erasmus's opponents, summoned a conference at Valladolid to pronounce upon his orthodoxy. Although the conference ended inconclusively, Manrique hastened to forbid any more attacks on Erasmus, and it seemed that the Erasmians had triumphed. But the conservatives were not prepared to acknowledge defeat. By introducing an element of doubt about the orthodoxy of Erasmus they had already succeeded in putting their opponents on the defensive, and an opportunity soon presented itself for resuming the attack when Charles V—the great patron of the Erasmians—left for Italy in 1529. This time the anti-Erasmians adopted the device of accusing the Erasmians of Illuminism[2] and Lutheranism. They received invaluable assistance from a certain Francisco Hernández, formerly the director of the *Alumbrados* of Valladolid, who turned informer after his arrest, and denounced, one after another, the leading Erasmians in Spain. Armed with this useful testimony the Inquisition felt itself strong enough to bring to trial certain influential Erasmians, including the famous Valdés brothers and Miguel de Eguía, the printer of Erasmus's works at Alcalá. The series of trials reached its climax in 1533 with that of the Greek scholar Juan de Vergara, a friend of Erasmus and a leading personality in Spanish humanist circles. Denounced as an Illuminist and a Lutheran by Hernández, Vergara was compelled in 1535 to abjure his sins publicly in an *auto de fe* and to spend a year in the seclusion of a monastery.

"The campaign to smear Erasmianism by linking it with Lutheran and Illuminist heresies was brilliantly successful, and the condemnation of Vergara virtually put an end to the Spanish Erasmian movement. Some Erasmians, like Pedro de Lerma, abandoned Spain, where they saw no future for scholarship and learning, while others were rounded up during the later 1530s. They, like their colleagues in other parts of Europe, were in effect victims of the times in which they lived—exponents of a

[2] Illuminism (the *alumbrados*) was an occasionally unorthodox style of Spanish mysticism.

tolerant humanist tradition which was everywhere collapsing before the advance of religious dogmatism. But they were also victims of the particular situation inside Spain, where the intermingling of Christians, Jews, and Moors had created religious and racial problems of unparalleled complexity and had prompted the organization of a tribunal dedicated to a solution along the only lines that seemed feasible—the imposition of orthodoxy. The Spanish Inquisition, operating in a land where heterodox views abounded and where the new heresies might therefore easily take root, was naturally terrified at the least hint of subversive practices, and dared not tolerate even the slightest deviation from the most rigid orthodoxy, in the fear that any deviation would open the way to greater heresies. For if the friars who ran the Inquisition were animated by hatred of alien beliefs, they also acted under the impulse of fear. The Holy Office was essentially the product of fear—and inevitably, being the product of fear, it was on fear that it flourished. In the 1530's and 1540's it transformed itself into a great apparatus operating through delation and denunciation—a terrible machine that would eventually escape from the control of its own creators and acquire an independent existence of its own. Even if, as seems probable, most Spaniards had come by the middle of the sixteenth century to consider the Holy Office as a necessary protection—a 'heaven-sent remedy', as Mariana[3] called it—this does not necessarily imply that they were not terrified of it. Fear bred fear, and it was a measure of the propaganda success of the Inquisition that it persuaded the populace to fear heresy even more than the institution which was designed to extirpate it.

"The features of the Inquisition most notorious in popular accounts of its activities were often less exceptionable in the contemporary context than is sometimes assumed. Torture and burning for the sake of one's beliefs were not, after all, practices exclusive to Spain; and—even if this was scarcely a source of much consolation to the victims—the methods of torture employed by the Holy Office were on the whole, traditional, and

---

[3] Juan de Mariana (1535–1623) was a great Jesuit historian and political theorist. He was not, however, consistent, and attacked its excesses, too.

did not run to the novel refinements popularly imagined. Great care was taken to ensure a 'just' verdict, and the death sentence appears to have constituted only a small proportion of the many sentences given. Unfortunately it is impossible to discover the total number of victims burnt for heresy. The figures were probably high for the first years of the tribunal's life—the chronicler of the Catholic Kings, Hernando de Pulgar, speaks of nearly 2000 men and women—but seem to have dropped sharply in the sixteenth century.

"While burning and torture were in no sense the exclusive prerogative of the Spanish Inquisition, the tribunal did, on the other hand, possess certain distinctive features which made it particularly objectionable. There was, first, the secrecy and the interminable delay of its proceedings: Fray Luis de León (1527-91) was kept for five years in the cells of the Inquisition awaiting his verdict. There was also the indelible stain which imprisonment inflicted not simply on the reputation of the accused himself, but on the reputation of his descendants also. Nor did he lose only his honour. One of the principal reasons for fear of the Inquisition was to be found in its right to confiscate the property of those who were penanced. "Reconciliation" therefore meant economic as well as social ruin—and consequently innumerable opportunities of blackmail for unscrupulous officials of the Holy Office.

"Of all the obnoxious features of the Inquisition, however, perhaps the most obnoxious was its natural tendency to generate a climate of mistrust and mutual suspicion peculiarly propitious for the informer and the spy. There were some 20,000 familiars through Spain, ever on the alert for manifestations of unorthodoxy; and their activities were supplemented by the unpleasant device known as the Edict of the Faith, by which inquisitors would visit a district at regular intervals and would have a list of heretical and obnoxious practices read to the assembled population. The reading would be followed by an exhortation to the hearers to denounce any such practices as had come to their knowledge, with severe penalties being threatened to those who kept silent. Since victims of the Inquisition were never informed of the identity of their accusers, the Edict of Faith presented an ideal opportunity for the settlement of private scores, and encouraged informing and delation as a matter of course. 'The gravest thing of all', wrote Mariana, ostensibly reporting the opinion of others, but perhaps expressing his own, "was that through these secret inquiries people were deprived of the liberty of listening and talking to one another, for there were in the cities, towns, and villages special persons to give warning of what was happening. . . .'

"In this climate of fear and suspicion, vigorous debate was checked and a new constraint made itself felt. Even if the Holy Office did not interfere directly with most secular works, the effects of its activities could not be confined exclusively to the theological sphere, which was technically its sole concern. Authors, even of non-theological works, would naturally tend to exercise a kind of self-censorship, if only to keep their writings free of anything that might mislead the ignorant and the uneducated, and furnish an additional weapon to enemies of the Faith. Consequently there was a new spirit of caution abroad, which inevitably inhibited the wide-ranging debate and inquiry that had characterized the reign of the Catholic Kings.

"It would be wrong, however, to assume that the Inquisition was the sole source of constraint in sixteenth-century Spain, or that it introduced entirely new features into Spanish life. Indeed, it may have taken such firm hold of Spanish society precisely because it gave official sanction to already existing attitudes and practices. Suspicion of those who deviated from the common norm was deeply rooted in a country where deviation was itself more normal than elsewhere—and a man could be suspect for his race as well as for his faith. It is no coincidence that the rise of a tribunal intended to impose religious orthodoxy was accompanied by the growth of certain practices designed to secure racial purity, for religious and racial deviation were easily equated in the popular mind. Indeed, alongside the obsessive concern with purity of the faith there flourished a no less obsessive concern with purity of blood; both obsessions were at their most violent in the middle decades of the sixteenth century; both employed the same techniques of informing and delation; and both had the effect of narrowing the extraordinarily wide range of Spanish life, and of forcing a rich and vital society into a strait-jacket of conformity."

2   *Miguel de la Pinta Llorente*
             A Spanish Catholic View

*The following is excerpted from one of the more recent general
surveys of the Inquisition in the traditional and conservative Spanish
view that the tribunal basically saved Spain from the various shortcomings of modern, secular society. Pinta Llorente, on the other
hand, is not unaware of Spain's own shortcomings, stemming from
her relative isolation from the main currents of European developments after about the middle of the sixteenth century. At the same
time, he is ideologically compelled, as it were, to attack those events
most responsible for modern "errors," such as the Renaissance and
the Enlightenment; he is thereby reduced to moralistic and hortatory
explanations for Spain's failures, as the selections demonstrate. Much
more openly than his predecessors in this line of argument then, he
confronts the fact that Spain was and is not perfect or, by national
definition, superior to the rest of western Europe. Pinta Llorente
remains, so to speak, uncomfortably on the horns of this classic
dilemma, perhaps to some small extent immediately foreshadowing
the current ferment among the Spanish clergy. It is also worth notic-
ing this author's very pessimistic view of man, as shown by his
remarks on censorship and authority, which perhaps also reflect the
state of the Franco government just after the second world war,
when church and state seemed ideologically united. His continuing
attacks on such "free-thinking" movements as the Renaissance and
the Enlightenment are therefore hardly surprising. Yet in his more
specialized investigations he is far more judicious and scholarly: his
writings constitute an oddly contradictory flow.*

SOURCE. Miguel de la Pinta Llorente, *La Inquisicion Española y los
Problemas de la Cultura y de la Intolerancia*, Vol. I (Madrid: Ediciones
Cultura Hispanica, 1953), pp. 12, 56–57, 215–216, 279, 284, and 286.

I, p. 12: "One would have striven vainly to be a part of that great age of the Renaissance and marvelous geographical discoveries if the Holy Office had not devoted its gifts and powers to fight its dangerous aspects, contradictory fruits of science and heterodox conscience, frankly inadmissible from the Roman Catholic view . . . . [He stresses what he believed to be the inherent immorality, etc., of these retrograde, un-Catholic aspects and observes that all governments use necessary forms of repression and censorship to safeguard their peoples' morality and laws which he interprets as a necessary 'intolerance.']¹ . . . . This intolerance is old in the world and is exercised in all states and by all institutions in order to avoid that tragic decadence to which man could be degraded through immorality with all its human meanness and shame . . . in the press statutes and government censorship in modern nations, demanded by normalcy and political coherence of these lands in defence of their proper historical constitutions, their peculiar genius, and to bring about the definitive evaluation of the ecclesiastical *fiscalizarios* [ie., very broadly, church interpretation of censorship, etc.] . . . in the name of the holy patrimony of the faith. . . ."

I, 56-57. "The Expurgatory Indexes, that is to say, the Inquisition's censorship . . . signified unquestionably an intellectual regimen which pressed to proclaim and establish in the European countries [a] midway between religious dissidence . . . and secularizing humanism, rationalist and atheistic . . . [He then relates this 'middle way' to 20th century Spain, with obvious satisfaction.]"

I, 215. "The Protestant dissolution of the theological spirit was among the antecedents of this pretended [i.e., claimed or attempted] renovation [the 18th century Enlightenment, etc.]."

I, 216. The new man, even in Spain, was "meditative and skeptical. It was the epoch of superficiality and levity, abounding in literary artifice and frivolous games [; certainly not] in philosophical irony or cool analysis."

---

¹ The numerous bracketed statement in this selection are regrettably necessary in order to sum up the author's occasionally tediously put but relevant comments.

I, 215. Pinta Llorente sees the age of Louis XIV producing a "skeptical and irreligious movement." The other contributions to the war against the traditionally classic-French ideology came from "England, land of the Bible and the Common Law . . . [which after about 90 years of a civil war and revolutionary changes in the government and conduct] . . . then settled into an innovating and antitraditional movement—the reaction against the subordination of a man's intellect to morality . . . [He then, at great length, expostulates upon Voltaire as the most infamous case of such a development.]"

I, 279. Quotes from an earlier Spanish student of the subject: "The Spanish Inquisition was almost benign and philanthropic compared to tribunals of that age elsewhere" . . . and the accusation of another Spaniard that "a long list of scientists [i.e., intellectuals in general] perished in its dungeons is merely a concession to the gallery . . . ." Pinta Llorente refutes as entirely false. [He actually seems to mean no *Catholic* savant was so treated, and repudiates the old notion that the Inquisition sapped Spanish intellectual energies and personnel. On page 280 he observes that such men manned the Holy Office's front ranks and cites a "liberal and modern man," Juan de Valera, who pointed out that the Spanish greatness of the 16th and 17th centuries coincided with the Inquisition's era of greatest power. Ed.] While subsequently delineating Menéndez Pelayo's[2] well-known attitudes in this area, he again cites the 'progressive' Valera on p. 281 on the Spanish decadence, due to "an epidemic, which infected the nation's virile majesty. It was a fever of pride, a delirium of arrogance [from prosperity and the euphoria attending the end of the Reconquest]. We were filled with haughty disdain and Jewish fanaticism. From here stems our divorce and isolation from the rest of Europe." [Pinta Llorente adds that much of the clerical and lay elite unsuccessfully fought these developments and is aware, correctly, that such attitudes reflected popular Spanish feelings, which in turn suggests that the Inquisition itself, in the main, accurately reflected popular views and did not necessarily initiate them. Pinta Llorente's accuracy here is not accompanied by any serious

[2] See introduction for extended comments.

notion that there was something tragic or amiss in all of this.
Ed.]

I, 284. On the prosecution of Luis de Léon and other biblical
scholars in late 16th century Castile: "The process revealed a
series of sensible limitations. . ." on such efforts concerning
the Bible, etc. [Léon was jailed for five years before gaining
acquittal-Ed.]

I, 286. "The history of mankind is the history of intolerance
and the most radical intransigencies."

3   *R. Trevor Davies*
              A Non-Spanish Catholic View

P. 12. "In Spain racial purity and religious orthodoxy had
become mutually dependent. . . . The value of the Inquisition
as a royal instrument for strengthening the monarchy and
unifying the country would be difficult to exaggerate." [Cf.
Elliott.]

P. 13. "Furthermore, the Inquisition took no account of
those privileges of nobility and . . . extensive liberties and
franchises that were a perpetual embarrassment to the Crown.
It stood for social justice. It tended to reduce all men . . . to a
common level before the law . . . [and] could be used by the
Crown to achieve secular aims, in cases where the ordinary
courts were difficult to move, or where the laws and customs
. . . created difficulties. [Davies seems to be implicitly and
favourably comparing this tribunal with the English court of
the Star Chamber under the early Tudors.-Ed.] [Its] familiars
. . . exercising constant vigilance in the most remote regions
. . . may, indeed, fittingly be compared with those efficient
Justices of the Peace who did so much to support the throne in
Tudor England."

SOURCE. R. Trevor Davies, *Golden Century Of Spain, 1501–1621* (London-New York, Macmillan & Co., Ltd., 1961), pp. 12, 13, 16, and 135. Reprinted by permission of St. Martin's Press and Macmillan & Co., Ltd.

P. 16. "The popular appeal of the Inquisition was maintained by the periodical *auto de fe* [which] many ill-informed
writers have confused . . . with the burning of heretics . . . the
two things were quite distinct. The [latter] was carried out in
the ordinary place of execution as it was a matter for the secular arm, to which the heretics had been 'relaxed.' Berruguete's
[an artist] well-known picture of victims tied to a stake awaiting
their death by fire at an *auto* . . . has, apparently, little foundation in fact." [This, on the face of it, is an astounding remark.
Ed.]

P. 135. "Moreover, religious toleration can only exist when
a large body of public opinion is willing to accept it. No such
body . . . existed in Spain at the time nor, for that matter, in
any other part of Europe. . . . It so happened that Philip [II]
was able to do with the full consent of his conscience what
many other rulers, such as Queen Elizabeth . . . were doing
from political expediency alone. But had some such cynical
agnostic occupied . . . Spain, obvious expediency would have
compelled him to [Philip's] course."

[Note that while this is basically sound it is clearly marked by
the author's strong bias against Elizabethan England in favor of
Philip and Spain. Ed.]

4   *Henry Charles Lea*
      An Anglo-Saxon Protestant-Rationalist View

*As previously noted most students of the Inquisition still owe a
great debt to the labors of Henry Charles Lea. Yet as this brief but
revealing paragraph from Lea's introduction to his most famous work
shows, he was affected by a very well-defined set of controlling
assumptions. These, perhaps, were a sort of mirror image of those
from which Spanish Catholic apologists like Pinta Llorente worked.
It is hardly surprising that, from the first, many Spanish historians
were repelled by the condemnatory moralistic tone in Lea, for all
his undoubted and massive scholarship, and that they spent more*

time in dissecting his obvious biases than in confronting the real implications of his carefully assembled data.

I, v. Statement of purpose. ". . . to present the daily operation of a tribunal of which the real importance is to be sought, not so much in the awful solemnities of the *auto de fe,* or in the cases of a few celebrated victims, as in the silent influences exercised by its incessant and secret labors among the mass of the people and in the limitations which it placed on the Spanish intellect—in the resolute conservatism with which it held the nation in the medieval groove and unfitted it for . . . rational liberty when the nineteenth century brought the inevitable Revolution."

5   *Juan Antonio Llorente*
              A Spanish Anti-Clerical View

Juan Antonio Llorente was the first opponent of the Inquisition to buttress his arguments with something approaching the objective use of historical evidence. He was perhaps the first "scientific" critic of the tribunal, and was accepted as such in his own day. There can be little doubt, however, that in light of subsequent research, even by those more or less sharing Llorente's animus towards the Holy Office, he can no longer be considered reliable. His efforts, however, undoubtedly forced defenders of the Inquisition to confront the relevant sources more seriously, and also must have contributed greatly to the debate raging over the reinstatement of the tribunal in 1814, which ended in its definitive abolition in 1834. Clearly, Llorente also contributed substantially to the growing anticlerical tradition in Spain in

SOURCE. Henry Charles Lea, *A History Of The Inquisition In Spain* (New York-London, The Macmillan Company, 1906), I, v. Reprinted with permission of The Macmillan Company. Copyright 1906 by The MacMillan Company. Renewed 1934 by Arthur H. Lea.

the nineteenth century. He was also clearly an Erastian (an advocate of the subordination of church to state) as both his approach and selection of data show. The almost immediate translation of his work into several languages certainly added to the generally gloomy view of Spain then commonly held, and this affected substantially its reception among sensitive Spaniards.

From the translator's "Advertisement": "All the records of the fantastic cruelties of the heathen world do not afford so appalling a picture of human weakness and depravity as the . . . documents of the laws and proceedings of this Holy Office, which professed to act under the influence of the doctrine of the Redeemer of the World!"

Pp. XV-XIX. "This history will make known numberless attempts perpetrated by the inquisitors against magistrates who defended the rights of sovereign authority, in opposition to the enterprises of the *holy office* and the court of Rome; and which enables me to state the trials of many celebrated men and ministers who defended the prerogatives of the crown, and whose only crimes were having published works on the right of the crown, according with the the true principles of jurisprudence. These trials will display the Counsellors of the Inquisition carrying their audacity to such a height, as to deny that their temporal jurisdiction was derived from the concession on their sovereign, and actually prosecuting all the members of the council of Castile, as rash men, suspected of heresy, for having made known and denounced to the king this system of usurpation. In addition to these intolerable acts, will be found accounts of their assumption of superiority over viceroys, and other great officers of state. I have also shewn, that these ministers of persecution have been the chief causes of the decline of literature, and almost the annihilators of nearly all that could enlighten the people, by their ignorance, their blind submission

SOURCE. Juan Antonio Llorente, *A Critical History Of the Inquisition Of Spain* (Williamstown, Massachusetts: John Lilburne, Co., 1967). Reprinted from the abridged and anonymously translated English edition of 1823. One page from original translator's "Advertisement," pp. xv–xix, and pp. 323–325.

to the monks who were qualifiers, and by persecuting the magistrates and the learned who were anxious to disseminate information. These monks were despicable scholastic theologians, too ignorant and prejudiced to be able to ascertain the truth between the doctrines of Luther and those of Roman Catholicism, and so condemned, as Lutheran, propositions incontestably true.

"The horrid conduct of this *holy office* weakened the power and diminished the population of Spain, by arresting the progress of arts, sciences, industry, and commerce, and by compelling multitudes of families to abandon the kingdom; by instigating the expulsion of the Jews and the Moors; and by immolating on its flaming shambles more than *three hundred thousand victims!!* So replete with duplicity was the system of the inquisitors-general, and the council of this *holy office*, that if a papal bull was likely to circumscribe their power, or check their vengeance, they refused to obey, on the pretext of its being opposed to the laws of the kingdom, and the orders of the Spanish government. By a similar proceeding, they evaded the ordinances of the king, by alleging that papal bulls prevented them from obeying, under pain of excommunication.

"Secrecy, the foe of truth and justice, was the soul of the tribunal of the Inquisition; it gave to it new life and vigour, sustained and strengthened its arbitrary power, and so emboldened it, that it had the hardihood to arrest the highest and noblest in the land, and enabled it to deceive, by concealing facts, popes, kings, viceroys, and all invested with authority by their sovereign. This *holy office*, veiled by secrecy, unhesitatingly kept back, falsified, concealed, or forged the reports of trials, when compelled to open their archives to popes or kings. The Inquisitors constantly succeeded, by this detestable knavery, in concealing the truth, and facilitated their object by being careful not to number the reports. This was practised to a great extent in the trials of the archbishop of Toledo, of the Prothonotary, and others.

"Facts prove beyond doubt, that the extirpation of Judaism was not the real cause, but the mere pretext, for the establishment of the Inquisition by Ferdinand V. The true motive was to carry on a vigorous system of confiscation against the Jews, and so bring their riches into the hands of the government. Sixtus IV sanctioned the measure, to gain the point dearest to the court of Rome, an extent of domination. Charles V protected it from motives of policy, being convinced it was the only means of preventing the heresy of Luther from penetrating into Spain. Philip II was actuated by superstition and tyranny to uphold it; and even extended its jurisdiction to the excise, and made the exporters of horses into France liable to seizure by the officers of the tribunal, as persons suspected of heresy! Philip III, Philip IV, and Charles II pursued the same course, stimulated by similar fanaticism and imbecility, when the re-union of Portugal to Spain led to the discovery of many Jews. Philip V maintained the Inquisition from considerations of mistaken policy, inherited from Louis XIV, who made him believe that such rigour would ensure the tranquillity of the Kingdom, which was always in danger when many religions were tolerated. Ferdinand VI and Charles III befriended this *holy office*, because they would not deviate from the course that their father had traced, and because the latter hated the freemasons. Lastly, Charles IV supported the tribunal, because the French Revolution seemed to justify a system of surveillance, and he found a firm support in the zeal of the inquisitors-general, always attentive to the preservation and extension of their power, as if the sovereign authority could find no surer means of strengthening the throne, then the terror inspired by an Inquisition.

"*During the time I remained in London, I heard some Catholic affirm that the Inquisition was useful in Spain, to preserve the Catholic faith, and that a similar establishment would have been useful in France.*

"These persons were deceived, by believing that it was sufficient for people to be good Catholics not to have any fear of the *holy office*. They knew not that nine-tenths of the prisoners were deemed guilty, though true to their faith, because the ignorance or malice of the denouncers prosecuted them for points of doctrine, which were not susceptible of heretical interpretation, but in the judgment of an illiterate monk, . . . considered erudite by the world, because he is said to have studied the theology of the schools. The Inquisition encouraged hypocrisy, and punished those who either did not know how, or would not, assume the mask. This tribunal wrought no conversion. The Jews and Moriscoes, who were baptized without being truly converted, merely that they might remain in Spain, are examples which prove the truth of this assertion. The former perished on the pyres of the Inquisition, the latter crossed over into Africa with the Moors, as much Mahometans as their ancestors were before they were baptised.

"I conclude with declaring, that the contents of this history are original, and that I have drawn my facts with fidelity, from the most authentic sources, and might have greatly extended them."

Pp. 323-325. "In addition to the prevention of the progress of literature, the Inquisition was so much dreaded by the magistrates, that criminals were frequently left unpunished. Ferdinand and his successors had granted privileges to this tribunal, which the encroachments of the inquisitors soon rendered insupportable. They even endeavoured to humiliate three sovereigns: Clement VIII [Rome-Ed.] at home; the Prince of Bearn, King of Navarre; and the Grand Master of the Order of St. John of Jerusalem, at Malta. They also attacked and qualified, as suspected of heresy, the whole Council of Castile; excited seditions in several cities by their arbitrary measures; and persecuted several members of their own *Supreme* Council.

"This system of domination has never been repressed either by the general laws of Spain and America, the particular resolutions taken in each of the kingdoms of the crown of Arragon, the king's ordinations, of the circular letters of the Council of the Inquisition. The inquisitors have been punished (though rarely) by being deprived of their offices; this, however, had no effect. Lastly, the general conventions have not been less important in restraining the ambition which led them to endeavour to establish their dominion throughout the world by fear.

"The Inquisition presents to our view a tribunal, whose judges have neither obeyed the laws of the kingdom in which it was established, the bulls of the Popes, the first constitutions of the tribunal, nor the particular orders of its chiefs; which has even dared to resist the power of the Pope, in whose name it acts, and has disowned the king's authority eleven different times; which has suffered books to circulate, favouring regicides and the authority of the Popes to dethrone kings, and at the same time condemned and prohibited works containing a contrary doctrine, and defending the rights of the sovereign; which acted in this manner in circumstances entirely foreign to the crime of heresy, which was the only one they were competent to judge. Some examples will be given of the contests for jurisdiction which have so much injured Spain.

"In 1553, the inquisitors of Calahorra excommunicated and arrested the licentiate Izquierdo, *alcalde-major* of Arnedo, for having attempted to prosecute Juan Escudero, a familiar of the *holy office*, who had assassinated a soldier. They also ordered divine service to cease at Arnedo. The Chancery of Valladolid demanded the writings of the trial, but the inquisitors eluded two of their ordinances. In the mean time the culprit was left at liberty in the town of Calahorra, and afterwards make his escape, so that the crime remained unpunished.

"In 1567, the inquisitors of Murcia excommunicated the Chapter of the Cathedral, and the municipality of that city; their competence was contested, and the Supreme Council decided that some members of the chapter and municipality should make public reparation in the capital of the kingdom, and receive absolution; they received it in public, and in the character of penitents, before the altar.

"In 1568, a royal ordinance prescribed the execution of the Convention, known as that of *Cardinal Espinoza*. It was issued, on the inquisitors of Valencia claiming the right of judging in affairs concerning the police of the city and many others, such as contributions, smuggling, trade, etc. They asserted that this right belonged to them, particularly if one of the individuals concerned in the affair was in the service of the Inquisition. They would not allow any criminal to be arrested in the houses of the inquisitors either in the town or country, while even the churches were no longer a refuge for those they pursued.

"In 1569, the tribunal of Barcelona excommunicated and imprisoned the military deputy and the civil vice-governor of the city, and several of their people. Their crime was, having exacted from an usher of the Inquisition a certain privilege called *la Merchandise*. The royal Council of Arragon contested the competence of the Council of the Inquisition; but Philip II put an end to the dispute, by liberating the prisoners: the inquisitors were not punished for disobeying the law, which forbids them to excommunicate a magistrate."

6 *Henry Kamen*
A Marxist View

Henry Kamen has remarked of himself that he is both a Catholic in religion and a Marxist in philosophy. There seems little or none of the former in his discussion of the Inquisition, but quite a bit of the latter. This author's emphasis on class struggles as perhaps the most vital aspect of the Inquisition's foundation, support, and spread, in the form of attacking the basically Jewish and Marrano bourgeoisie, is, to say the least, quite controversial and debatable. But certainly Kamen has enlivened the debate over such problems revolving about the tribunal with his fresh if somewhat tenuous views.

In his book, Kamen begins by stating that he views his work as an effort not designed to give "an account of the Inquisition so much as a tentative interpretation of its place in Spanish history" (p. ix). He then briefly traces developments in late medieval Spain, particularly Castile, culminating in the dynastic union of the latter with the Crowns of Aragon, through Ferdinand and Isabella's marriage, and then the ending of the last independent Muslim entity in Granada in 1492. He stresses, especially for the central and dominant Castilian partner, the unchecked power of the nobility and the growing anti-Semitism, both, he thinks, largely a consequence of the increasingly favorable military-political situation for the Christians from the late middle ages. He sees the previous "open" society as the result chiefly of the absence of Muslim or Christian power in relatively total, absolute terms.

SOURCE. Henry Kamen, *The Spanish Inquisition* (London-New York: George Weidenfeld & Nicolson, Ltd., 1965), pp. 3–5, 7–8, 202, and 208–209. Reprinted by permission of George Weidenfeld & Nicolson, Ltd., The New American Library, Inc., and the author.

P. 3. "What made the situation in the fourteenth century
[and from then] different was that 'it was no longer possible
for Christians, Moors, and Jews to live under the same roof,
because the Christian now felt himself strong enough to break
down the traditional custom of Spain whereby the Christian
population made war and tilled the soil, the Moor built the
houses, and the Jew presided over enterprise as a fiscal agent
and skilled technician.' [Kamen here cites Castro's *Structure of
Spanish History*, p. 225, and appears to accept this rather overly
sharp demarcation of occupations supposedly marking the earlier,
"open" period. Ed.] In this way the possibility that Spain might
see the evolution of a multi-racial [and religious] society based
on mutual tolerance was explicitly rejected by the men who now
came to rule the peninsula . . .

Pp. 4-5. ". . . The Catholic monarchs have usually been
credited with reducing the power and influence of these classes
[the upper clergy and nobility—Kamen then outlines processes
illustrating rather how Ferdinand and Isabella further solidified
their socioeconomic power while superficially seeming to
weaken their political-military strength]. . . . This followed the
general trend in western Europe, where the rise of the new
monarchies was based on alliances with the feudal nobility
against the urban middle classes. The results of this policy in
Castile . . . directly concern us, for it was events in Castile
that led to the rise of the modern Spanish Inquisition. . . ."
[This reflects recent research and interpretations, altering the
traditional view of the "new monarchies." Ed.]

P. 7. ". . . The importance of 1492 [the expulsion of all
unconverted Jews from all Spain] then, consists not in the
expulsion itself but in its historical context. [It] was, in its
widest interpretation, an attempt by the feudalistic nobility to
eliminate that section of the middle classes—the Jews—which
was threatening its predominance in the state. It was a refusal
of the old order to accept the new importance of those sections
of the community that controlled the capital and commerce of
the towns. This reaction . . . [had first] developed during the
fourteenth century, at the very time that the Christian recon-
quests of the thirteenth . . . had destroyed racial co-existence

. . . Thus the consciousness of conflicting interests came to the fore at the same time as a sharpened awareness of the potential religious and racial danger presented by the two great Jewish and Moorish minorities in Spain. . .

P. 8. [After noting that 1492 solved little and, rather, merely enormously added to the already-suspect converso class, whose Christian "unreliability" had led to the Inquisition's creation in 1478, Kamen continues] ". . . the Inquisition continued to function with renewed vigor. What emerges from this situation is that [it] was neither more nor less than a class weapon, used to impose on all communities of the peninsula the ideology of one class—the lay and ecclesiastical aristocracy. Their beliefs and ideals were to be the norm of Castilian life. . . ."

[To be fair to this author, at other places in this work, he is well aware that the Inquisition reflected popular Spanish ideals and prejudices, and often served as much to confirm as to implant them. Ed.]

P. 202. On the tribunal's comparatively lenient and enlightened attitude towards witchcraft: "Sixtus V . . . in 1585 . . . condemned all astrology, magic, and demonology. The progressive attitude of the papacy and the Inquisition in this matter is worth stressing, because astrology was accepted throughout Europe, in even the most learned circles, as a legitimate science. . . ."

[But with Alonso de Salazar Frias's report on this problem in 1612, "a monument to the triumph of reason over superstition," wisdom was and remained victorious.] Pages 208-209. ". . . Salazar came to his astounding conclusion:

"Considering the above with all the Christian attention in my power, I have not found even indications from which to infer that a single act of witchcraft has really occurred . . . three-quarters and more have accused themselves and their accomplices falsely . . . they would freely . . . revoke their confessions if they thought . . . they would be received kindly without punishment [by the inquisitors] . . . [who] with increasing zeal are discovering every hour more witches . . . I also feel that . . . in the diseased state of the public mind, every agitation of the matter is harmful and increases the evil. I deduce the importance of silence and reserve from the experience that *there were neither witches nor bewitched until they were talked and written about.* [Kamen's italics]. . . ."

[It remains somewhat curious that this tribunal came to go by rules which ended by discrediting witchcraft and the like, which if similarly applied to other areas might well have had more disinterested results concerning Judaism, etc. On witchcraft generally, see Julio Caro Baroja, *The World of Witches* (Chicago and London: University of Chicago Press and Geo. Weidenfeld & Nicolson, Ltd., 1964; O.N. V. Glendinning, translator). In a two-part essay in the May and June 1967 numbers of *Encounter*, H.R. Trevor-Roper, "The Witch Craze," (reprinted in *The European Witch Craze and Other Essays*, Harper Torchbk., 1969) tries to place this phenomenon in its broadest historical (and geographic) European setting. Rarely has this editor read so stimulating an article, which nonetheless merits the warning: "Read cautiously." Trevor-Roper believes firmly that the sole cause of the Spanish Inquisition's relative sanity regarding witchcraft was because it (and Spain generally) already had sufficient scapegoats in the conversos, Moriscos, Judaizers, et al. This strikes me as much too pat, although to be sure, I claim to no expertise or really solid knowledge on which to base a serious analysis. But see the forthcoming volume in this series by Professor E. William Monter of Northwestern University on witchcraft and related matters, primarily in this same early modern era. Ed.]

7   *B. Netanyahu*
A Controversial Jewish View

It is relatively rare to have accessible Jewish or Israeli scholarship in an endeavor such as this. For this reason I have included very lengthy selections from Netanyahu's recent analysis of why the Spanish Marranos by and large fell away from Judaism from the late middle ages. It is to be stressed that Israeli and non-Israeli Jewish scholars have severely judged much of Netanyahu's handling of his data and his interpretations. Historiographically this author, in trying to explain why the large Spanish Hebrew community proved so vulnerable to Christianization when others stood firm in martyrdom, massacre, and exile, in often similar circumstances, ends up curiously in the camp of the Spanish Catholic polemicist. Netanyahu's villain, if we may use the word here, is the secularizing philosophical current of the 14th and 15th centuries which, in the hands of younger radicals of the community's elite, eroded the mainstays of Judaism which traditionally had sustained the faith against conversion, whether by persuasion or force. No doubt the arguments revolving about this approach have at least as much to do with contemporary Judaism, in and out of Israel, as with the Spanish Marranos and the Inquisition. In any event, the parallel between Netanyahu's attack on the evils of an earlier philosophical radicalism and the conservative view of such movements as the Renaissance as dangerously secular and modernist, is striking. In conclusion, while much of the author's discussion concerns the decades preceding the Inquisition's founding, as background to that event and its subsequent history, his efforts have considerable merit. Netanyahu's view on the "non-Jewishness" of the conversos ought to be compared with the considerable Judaizing among them evidenced in the Baer documents.

Pp. 1-4. "One of the still unsettled questions related to Spanish-Jewish history is the measure of Jewishness to be attributed to the Marranos at various periods of the 15th century. Since both Spanish and Hispano-Jewish history are closely bound with the history of the Marranos, any answer given to this question necessarily bears upon our interpretation of much of what transpired in Christian Spain in that era. It is especially so when we consider the developments in the century's last three decades, for then we are confronted with two momentous events that were intimately connected with the Marrano problem. The first was the establishment of the Inquisition, whose avowed and, originally, sole purpose was to solve that problem

SOURCE. B. Netanyahu, *The Marranos of Spain: From The Late 14th To The Early 16th Century* (New York: American Academy For Jewish Research, 1966) pp. 1–4, 21, 97, 104–105, 188–189, 208, 233–234, 241–242, 245. Reprinted by permission of publisher and author.

in its own prescribed manner; the second was the expulsion of the Jews from Spain and the territories then controlled by it—a measure officially defended on the ground that the presence of the Jews in those countries was a factor militating against that solution. What is more, as the Edict of Expulsion indicates, the Inquisition was instrumental in procuring that measure, and thus the major events referred to were linked with each other in more ways than one; both stemmed from the same source: the forces that occasioned the establishment of the Inquisition and steered its course of action.

"Now, it is on the assumed Jewishness of the Marranos that the whole case of the Inquisition rests. Therefore, the results of our inquiry must touch, among other things, upon the moral and practical impulses of the entire inquisitorial drive. To realize how far-reaching are the implications of some of the possible conclusions, it is sufficient to reflect, even in a cursory manner, upon the following two alternatives. If the Marranos, or most of them, were Jews, as the advocates of the Inquisition have repeatedly claimed, one may censure the practices of the Inquisition, but one cannot negate a moral basis for its activities —at least, from a medieval point of view; more clearly, one may rightly maintain that in its struggle with the Jewish "heresy" the Inquisition showed excessive zeal, perhaps even undue virulence and rancor, but one cannot deny all justice to those who, being aware of that 'heresy', saw the need for *some* form of struggle, and thus one can hardly question the basic honesty of the Inquisition's declared aims. If, however, the assumption made regarding the Jewishness of the Marranos is wrong, it can hardly be claimed that the Inquisition was, or could for long remain, unaware of this fact. Consequently, we must seek other reasons—apart from those officially announced —both for the establishment of the Inquisition and the partic- ular policies it pursued. How Jewish were the Marranos? Indeed, upon the answer to this question depends not only our correct understanding of the motives, goals, and procedures of the Holy Office, but also the proper reconstruction of what truly hap- pened in Spain at that crucial period of Spanish and Jewish history.

"Jewish historians have, on the whole, accepted the first proposition, namely, that the Marranos, or most of them, were Jews. On the general reasons for this stand, as well as on its relationship to Spanish and other historical writings on the Inquisition, we have dwelt in considerable detail elsewhere. Here we shall limit ourselves to presenting the most extreme view expressed on the question, i. e., that of Professor Baer. As Baer sees it, 'the majority of the conversos were real Jews' and although this is a clear-cut statement, it may be further elucidated by Baer's additional and even more sweeping assertion: 'Conversos and Jews were *one people*, bound together by ties of religion, and fate, and messianic hope.' Accordingly, Baer does not hesitate to say that 'essentially the Inquisition was right in evaluating the character of the conversos.'[1]

"From this view I differ radically. I adhere to the hypothesis I had advanced elsewhere that (1) 'the overwhelming majority of the Marranos' at the time of the establishment of the Inquisition were not Jews, but detached from Judaism, or rather, to put it more clearly, Christians; (2) that 'in seeking to identify the whole Marrano group with a secret Jewish heresy, the Spanish Inquisition was operating with a fiction,' and (3) that 'it was driven to this operation by racial hatred and political considerations rather than by religious zeal.'

"On all these statements I still stand—in fact, I am now convinced of their veracity more than ever. What I can now add by way of clarification, and am better able to substantiate, is that the minority that still adhered to Judaism in the three decades preceeding the establishment of the Inquisition was, save for temporary and inconsequential reactions, constantly diminishing in size and influence; that it would have, in all likelihood, soon faded into nothingness, had not the process of assimilation been violently interfered with by the repellent and bewildering actions of the Inquisition; and that thus it was due to the Inquisition itself that the dying Marranism in Spain was given a new lease on life. As I see it, therefore, what actually happened was the reverse of what is generally assumed: *it was not a powerful Marrano movement that provoked the establish-*

---

[1] He refers to Baer's two-volume general history of the Spanish Jews, not the collection of documents; see Introduction.

ment of the Inquisition, but it was the establishment of the Inquisition that caused the temporary resurgence of the Spanish Marrano movement.

"If this hypothesis is correct, my contention that the Inquisition was based upon, and operated with, a fictitious charge must emerge as a necessary conclusion. And, what must be equally obvious in this event is that this fiction was in no way a product of misinformation or self-delusion, but of deliberate and careful calculation. If the case as presented by the Holy Office grossly exaggerated a situation which was in itself quite insignificant, those who used these tactics knew precisely what they were doing. The fact that there was a striking difference between the official campaign slogans of the Inquisition and the real, unpublished aims of its advocates should surprise no one at all familiar with the history of persecution. Campaign slogans of mass persecution movements rarely agree with their actual aims since persecution habitually claims, in self-justification, motives more noble than those that prompted it. Now, religious motivation, however distorted, has always some nobility to it, and in the Middle Ages in particular it had, besides an appeal, also an explosive force. That it was brought to the fore in the campaign against the Marranos was, therefore, merely part of a *modus operandi*, a means for attaining a certain end; but it was not really the religion of the Marranos with which the Inquisition was concerned. Its concern were the *bearers* of that religion. Its purpose was to degrade, impoverish, and ruin the influence of the Marranos in all spheres of life, to terrorize and demoralize them individually and collectively—in brief, to destroy them psychologically and physically so as to make it impossible for them to rise again as a factor of any consequence in Spain. The aim of the Inquisition, therefore, as I see it, was *not to eradicate a Jewish heresy from the midst of the Marrano group, but to eradicate the Marrano group from the midst of the Spanish people.*

"All these contentions represent so radical a departure from the theories hitherto accepted as valid, that their foundation—namely, the non-Jewishness of the Marranos, or at least of their overwhelming majority—must be conclusively proven before they can claim to be something more than a mere hypothesis, however plausible. When I first advanced this hypothesis, I supported it by a number of proofs and arguments that appeared to me cogent and decisive. Yet, an all-inclusive examination and analysis of the sources related to this question—both Jewish—was obviously called for. What I could not do in the framework of a biography, I propose to do here. The present study represents the first portion of the task at hand."

P. 21. "Regarding the special characteristics of the converted Jews vis-à-vis the unconverted, following the waves of mass conversions after the 1391 explosions[2]: "Here [in Christian Spain], neither the *minority* nor the *whole* community was converted, but the *majority*, and possibly the overwhelming one. Backed by the performance of the majority body which included many, or most, of the community's leaders, the ordinary forced convert in Spain could hardly develop feelings of shame or regret, the action of the majority tending to bolster his natural tendency to self-justification. Here, therefore, if the minority looked down upon him, or regarded him with disdain or reproach, it would become automatically subject to *his* censure, if not to his reciprocal scorn and aversion."

In a key footnote on this same page Netanyahu observes that the above generalizations refer to the post-1415 conditions, for "after 1391, however, while possibly counting a quarter of a million, the converts were not the majority of Spain's Jewry. Nevertheless, even then, since they were a *large minority* and constituted a powerful group, their condition differed in this respect from that of forced converts in Germany, for instance. Furthermore, also after 1391, the forced converts in Spain formed the *majority in a number* of important urban or regional communities, as, for instance, in Seville and Valencia [documentary citations follow]."

P. 97. "Faith in Judaism had been *shattered* before it was abandoned; and what had shattered that faith, at least in the initial stages, was not Christianity, but the thorough-going, long-

---

[2] The 1391 anti-Jewish riots in Seville, etc., which started the great waves of mass conversion.

lasting, and corruptive influence of secular philosophy." [Here he means precisely that basically Aristotelian rationalism which Aquinas had "Christianized" in the 13th century. Ed.]

Pp. 104-105. "Alami [a 15th century figure] points to the process of thought which links philosophy to conversion. The sum total of contemporary Spanish Jewish (Maimonides, et al.) philosophical thinking, namely, that the commandments were promulgated for the sole purpose of helping man attain intellectual exaltation, and that they are therefore not an 'end' but a 'means,' at once relegates the biblical precepts, the backbone of Judaism, to a mere secondary position. [There then ensues a stress on abstract speculation and reasoning powers, with the necessity of concentration and peace of mind] . . . if *this* is what secures man's perfection . . . why should he exert himself in the performance of the commandments under *all* circumstances and at *all* costs? Surely there is no point at all laying down his life [in martyrdom both meaningless and "old-fashioned"] . . . A means . . . when it proves to be a detriment, it should be abandoned. [If practicing Judaism causes suffering and deprives one] of the peace of mind essential for the development of his reasoning capacity . . . thus distracts [one] from his main goal[,] the inevitable conclusion of all this is quite obvious. To attain the highest [philosophic-rationalist] aim, Judaism may be helpful under *normal* circumstances; [otherwise] . . . it proves to be an obstacle that must be removed.

This . . . logic . . . leads inevitably from philosophy to conversion . . . [although], Alami admits, that the initiators of this course did not aim at that result. [They aimed at a Jewish-style reconciliation of mutually supporting faith and reason, in the modes of Maimonides and Aquinas; but the unintended and unavoidable upshot was the downgrading of Judaism.] . . . these people . . . , vile and villainous persons, whom Alami considers even more harmful to Jewry than both the Moslems and the Christians, served as an example to most [Jewish] notables . . . The flock, too, was soon affected by the shepherds, and in due course followed the same path."

Netanyahu describes conditions revolving about the Inquisition's inaugural and unfolding from 1478:

Pp. 188-189. "The acts of the few Marranos who leaned

towards Judaism led the gentiles to accuse the entire group as consisting of Judaizers and violators of Christian laws . . . these charges were . . . pressed against . . . many thousands of Marranos—in fact, all . . . and to this extent were groundless and libellous . . . the conversos [indeed had] 'endeavored to be like real gentiles' and . . . the name Israelite was foisted upon them . . . their flight from their native lands, their emergence from among the Christians, and consequently their return . . . resulted from 'compulsion and fear of death,' i.e., were an outcome of the Inquisition's terrors. *No element of their own free will was involved in this crucial development* . . .

". . . this remarkable [contemporary] statement [confirms the] thesis that the trend toward Judaism among the Marranos, noticeable after the establishment of the Inquisition, was not the product of an underground movement . . . but of the Inquisition itself; . . . without roots . . . entirely an outgrowth of external pressures. The Marranos, catapulted out of Christiandom, were a kind of death . . . Their re-embracing of Judaism . . . was really not a matter of choice, but . . . of choicelessness . . . ."

P. 208. "This brings our evidence to its summit, as well as to its conclusion. For as to the rest, i.e.. the *reasons* for the hostility manifested in the Inquisition's actions, our sources suggest no answer that we may consider historical. All they offer us is the theological interpretation, namely, that this hostility was a product of God's will, of his preordained plan, a punishment for the Marranos' betrayal, and the like. We shall get a clearer insight into the motives of the persecution when we turn to the non-Hebrew sources of the period. But a *hint* of its causes may also be found in the following address of the Jewish people to God, as formulated by Isaac Arama:

" 'You, God, know, and You are my witness, that in all the evils they have perpetrated against me, and in all the acts of veneance they have wrought upon me, *their sole intent was to annihilate and destroy me not because of my sins, but because of what I am.*' "

"Perhaps what Arama said about the Jews could be extended to the Marranos."

Amplification of the Marranos' situation after 1449 and why some looked back at Judaism favorably]:

Pp. 233-234. [This clandestine group appeared within the comparatively well-assimilated Marrano camp just after the great anti-Marrano pogrom at Toledo in the summer of 1467; another followed at Cordoba in 1473.] It was inevitable that the massacre and the accompanying campaign, . . . incessantly calling for their total destruction, would cause some . . . Marranos to [ultimately Judaize] . . . . The group must have been very small . . . perhaps limited merely to espousers of 'theoretical Judaism' [which apparently drew strong criticism from among publicly orthodox Jews] . . . [this] group remained extremely limited in scope and was in no way able to affect the broad current of Marrano life. But it was sufficient to give the Marrano-mongers *another* excuse for their agitation, and enable them to intensify their hue and cry about . . . 'Judaization' . . . [all of which] helped bring about a far greater persecution—that of the Inquisition."

[Netanyahu provides some interesting statistics]:

Pp. 241-242. "The size of the Marrano population of Spain [about 1480] was . . . somewhere between . . . 600,000 and . . . 1,000,000 . . . the Marrano population . . . constituted about 7%, and together with the Jewish community, less than 10% of the total population of Spain [which numbered about 9,250,000 by a 1482 census]." Page 245. "Thus, in view of all the above data and considerations, we arrive at the conclusion that the Marrano population of Spain in the 1480's was 600,000-700,000 strong . . . But . . . the . . . 'returners' . . . amounted . . . to a few thousand souls only, perhaps to a maximum of 6,000-7,000 within the first two decades of the Inquisition . . . no more than 1% of the total. And, if this was their number *after* the establishment of the Inquisition, we can gather the weakness of crypto-Judaism prior to [that]. Inexorably we [must conclude again] that the Inquisition was *not* established to wipe out a powerful and dangerous Jewish heresy . . . but for reasons altogether different."

[All italics in the above are the author's own. It must be stressed to the student that Netanyahu's view of these questions is his, and is by no means universally accepted by Jewish and

Israeli scholars. However, Netanyahu's work has the merit of
opening Inquisition issues from very different angles of approach
for the English-reading student. Ed.]

8   *F. Márquez Villanueva*
A Recent Scholarly Spanish View of the Conversos

*The following excerpt is from a recent article by one of the out-
standing younger Spanish students of the converso problem. Influ-
enced by the work of highly competent scholars such as Américo
Castro, Antonio Domínguez Ortiz, and Julio Caro Baroja, Márquez
Villanueva's efforts are marked by a consciously greater attempt, it
seems to me, to break away from traditional Spanish Catholic stereo-
typed thinking on this thorny topic and its equally allied and difficult
subjects, like the Inquisition itself. Indeed, in his hands, religion is
perhaps undervalued a bit too much.*

Pp. 318-320. "The conversos of 1391 were assimilated into
Christian society of the various Spanish kingdoms with incredible speed, without major difficulty, without grave incidences.
It is evident that the social structure of Spanish society already
in the early 15th century was characterized by a pronounced
demand for technicians in economic and bureaucratic activity
(accountants, estate managers, secretaries, municipal administra-
tors, etc.) because in no other way can the total lack of resistance
be explained when the conversos started to make nearly a
monopoly out of these professions. Old Christian Spain, concentrated on agriculture and . . . arms, found itself unable to
fill a vacuum of intellectual activity which became of greater

SOURCE. F. Márquez Villanueva, "The Converso Problem: An Assess-
ment," in *Collected Studies In Honor of Americo Castro's 80th Year*, M. P.
Hornik, editor (Oxford: Lincombe Lodge & Research Library, 1965), pp.
318–320. Reprinted by permission of the publisher.

importance every day. Precisely the fact that they were indispensable constituted the salvation and the tragedy of the
conversos . . . .

Up to the events of Toledo of 1449 [the first clear indication
of strong popular anticonverso feeling. Ed.], we have no serious
indications of opposition to the supremacy and social advance of
the New Christians . . . it showed that already one important
aspect of the social penetration of the conversos, their tendency
to monopolize the municipal administration, started to irritate
the proletarian masses. Difficulties in this field . . . [indeed
had] started already . . . in 1421. The anticonverso sentiment
of Spanish society started to crystallize around one of the
major social problems of European cities of the Late Middle
Ages: the conflict between the proletarian masses . . . and the
ruling *bourgeois* oligarchy, which, in fact, was already an
aristocracy.

During the second half of the 15th century the process of
economic transformation and the effects of the political chaos
[Castile was wracked by civil war, etc. during the reign of the
weak Henry IV, 1454–1474; Aragon suffered grave social-
political upheavals under John II, especially during 1462-1472.
Ed.] inflamed in an explosive degree the popular hatred of the
conversos. The proletarian mass believed to find the cause of all
its sufferings in the prosperity of the conversos, sometimes certainly scandalous, not taking into account that these were not
the cause of the new age, but only its most visible effect. The
rising tension, in fact, of this social conflict became visible in a
lamentable movement until it acquired the aspect of a religious
problem tending to justify the hatred by an alleged apostasy of
all New Christians.

"The ferment of this transformation with which all aspects of
the converso problem were connected, were the Mendicant
Orders [the begging monastic orders; i.e., the Franciscan and
Dominican Friars. Ed.], having close contact with the proletarian
mass out of which they also recruited their members [very
often].

". . . During the 15th century the conversos never acted as a
special group with its own personality and they never managed
to become identified, totally or as a majority, with one or

another of the groups and interests in permanent struggle against one another. They fully took part in all kinds of events and conflicts but in doing so they followed the general lines of development of Spanish society and they frequently clashed with conversos entrenched on the opposite side. In fact, not even the Inquisition was powerful enough to unite them in a common front. . . .

". . . it is not because we believe that the conscience of being Jewish was an essential element in their creation [the works of leading conversos like St. Teresa, et al.], and we neither believe that they were non-Spanish or just foreigners. We also do not believe as vulgar racialists or innocent believers would, that their Jewish origin or the fact of their conversion created in them a certain psychological structure or that it added anything or diminished anything in their creation.

". . . The intimate tragedy of the important conversos was not that they felt . . . Jewish amidst a gentile society, but in the painful experience to be submitted to injustice and suspicion by a religion and a society which seemed to them not to be sufficiently Christian . . . further, it is nothing but the tragedy of exquisite and select minorities who are . . . trampled on by masses which they should govern instead of being governed by . . . .

"The problem of the conversos acquires meaning only within the categories of Spanish life. There were always, and in appreciable numbers, converts of Judaism to Christianity in all parts of the world but only in Spain [do] we encounter a Santa Teresa . . . . All this can finally be traced back to . . . the easy assimilation of the Jews into Spanish society . . . ."

PART TWO

Sources and Trial Records

With Part Two the reader is confronted with segments of raw, primary data. In the sections by Baer, Schäfer, and Longhurst, original records of inquisitorial procedures and investigations are presented, virtually without comment or evaluation, by these scholars. The tone of the Roth excerpt and, more so, of the sixteenth century Spanish martyrology which concludes this book, is clearly designed to suggest strongly how the data should be interpreted by the reader. In this sense they link up directly with much of Part One, historiographically speaking. At the same time they remain primary material, in my judgment, and belong properly in this second part. The great French medievalist, Marc Bloch (1886-1944), said that at bottom history involved "confronting the sources." To fully comprehend an institution such as the Spanish Inquisition, which both reflected and furthered many basic values in Spain, Bloch's dictum is a minimal starting point, which too often has been insufficiently followed.

9   Cecil Roth
An Edict of Faith

The excerpt from Sir Cecil Roth's synthesis of the history of the Inquisition (in Portugal as well as Spain) show us a typical Edict of Faith (described generally in the Lynch selection). It might be pointed out that his work appeared between Hitler's accession to *power in Germany and the start of World War II. For a historian both English and Jewish, the 1930's were very grim indeed; and this effort must be understood as a product of that time, for much of this work is rather melodramatically done, including the presentation of documents, some of which were from apparently violently anti-inquisitorial sources.*

Pp. 76–85. "In the following, a typical 'Edict of Faith,' issued at Valencia in 1519, the prominence given to unimportant customs and mere superstitions is noteworthy.

" 'EDICT OF FAITH' "

" 'We Doctor Andres de Palacio, Inquisitor against the heresy and apostolic perversity in the city and kingdom of Valencia, etc.

" 'To all faithful Christians, both men and women, chaplains, friars and priests of every condition, quality and degree: whose attention to this will result in salvation in our Lord Jesus Christ, the true salvation; who are aware that, by means of other edicts and sentences of the Reverend inquisitors, our predecessors, they were warned to appear before them, within a given period, and declare and manifest the things which they had seen, known, and heard tell of any person or persons, either alive or dead, who had said or done anything against the Holy Catholic Faith; cultivated and observed the law of Moses or the Mohammedan sect, or the rites and ceremonies of the same; or perpetrated diverse crimes of heresy; observing Friday evenings and Saturdays; changing into clean personal linen on Saturdays and wearing better clothes than on other days; preparing on Fridays the food for Saturdays, in stewing pans on a small fire; who do not work on Friday evenings and Saturdays as on other days; who kindle lights in clean lamps with new wicks, on

SOURCE. Cecil Roth, *The Spanish Inquisition* (New York: W. W. Norton & Co., Inc., 1964), pp. 76–85. Reprinted by permission of publisher and author.

Friday evenings; place clean linen on the beds and clean napkins on the table; celebrate the festival of unleavened bread, eat unleavened bread and celery and bitter herbs; observe the fast of pardon (Day of Atonement) when they do not eat all day until the evening after star-rise, when they pardon one another and break their fast; and in the same manner observe the fasts of Queen Esther, of tissabav,[1] and resessena;[1] who say prayers according to the law of Moses, standing up before the wall, swaying back and forth, and taking a few steps backwards; who give money for oil for the Jewish temple or other secret place of worship, who slaughter poultry according to the Judaic law, and refrain from eating sheep or any other animal which is trefa; who do not wish to eat salt pork, hares, rabbits, snails, or fish that have not scales; who bathe the bodies of their dead and bury them in virgin soil according to the Jewish custom; who, in the house of mourning do not eat meat but fish and hard-boiled eggs, seated at low tables; who separate a morsel of dough when baking and throw it on the fire; who become, or know of others who become circumcised; who invoke demons, and give to them the honour that is due to God; who say that the law of Moses is good and can bring about their salvation; who perform many other rites and ceremonies of the same; who say that our Lord Jesus Christ was not the true Messiah promised in Scripture, not the true God nor son of God; who deny that he died to save the human race; deny the resurrection and his ascension to heaven; and say that our Lady the Virgin Mary was not the mother of God or a virgin before the nativity and after; who say and affirm many other heretical errors; who state that what they had confessed before the inquisitors was not the truth; who remove their penitential robes and neither remain in the prison nor observe the penance imposed upon them; who say scandalous things against our holy Catholic Faith and against the officials of the Inquisition; or who influence any infidel who might have been drawn towards Catholicism to refrain from converting; who assert that the Holy Sacrament of the altar is not the true body and blood of Jesus Christ our Redeemer, and that God cannot be omnipresent; or any priest

---

[1] Hebrew religious holidays.

holding this damnable opinion, who recites and celebrates the mass, not saying the holy words of the consecration; saying and believing that the law of Mahomet and its rites and ceremonies are good and can bring about their salvation; who affirm that life is but birth and death, and that there is no paradise and no hell; and state that to practise usury is no sin; if any man whose wife still lives, marries again, or any woman remarries in the lifetime of her first husband; if any know of those who keep Jewish customs, and name their children on the seventh night after their birth and with silver and gold upon a table, pleasurably observe the Jewish ceremony; and if any know that when somebody dies, they place a cup of water and a lighted candle and some napkins where the deceased died, and for some days, do not enter there; if any know of the effort of a Jew or convert, secretly to preach the law of Moses and convert others to this creed, teaching the ceremonies belonging to the same, giving information as to the dates of festivals and fasts, teaching Jewish prayers; if any know of anyone who attempts to become a Jew, or being Christian walks abroad in the costume of a Jew; if any know of anyone, converted or otherwise, who orders that his dress shall be made of canvas and not of linen, as the good Jews do; if any know of those who, when their children kiss their hands, place their hands on the children's heads without making the Sign (of the Cross); or who, after dinner or supper, bless the wine and pass it to everyone at the table, which blessing is called the veraha; if any know that in any house, people congregate for the purpose of carrying on religious services, or read out of bibles of the vernacular or perform other Judaic ceremonies, and if any know that when someone is about to set out on a journey, certain words of the law of Moses are spoken to him, and a hand placed on his head without making the Sign (of the Cross). And if any know of anyone who has professed the Mosaic creed, or awaited the coming of the Messiah, saying that our Redeemer and Saviour Jesus Christ was not come and that now Elijah was to come and take them to the promised land; and if any know that any person had pretended to go into a trance and wandered in heaven and that an angel had conducted him over green fields and told him that was promised land which was being saved for all converts whom Elijah was to redeem from the captivity in which they lived; and if any know that any person or persons be children or grandchildren of the condemned, and being disqualified, should make use of public office, or bear arms or wear silk and fine cloth, or ornament their costumes with gold, silver, pearls or other precious stones or coral, or make use of any other thing which they are forbidden and disqualified to have; and if any know that any persons have or possessed any confiscated goods, furniture, money, gold, silver, or other jewels belonging to those condemned for heresy, which should be brought before the receiver of goods confiscated for the crime of heresy. All these things, having been seen, heard or known, you, the above-mentioned faithful Christians, have, with obstinate hearts, refused to declare and manifest, greatly to the burden and prejudice of your souls; thinking that you were absolved by the bulls and indulgences issuued by our holy father, and by promises and donations which you had made, for which you have incurred the sentence of excommunication and other grave penalties under statutory law; and thus you may be proceeded against as those who have suffered excommunication and as abetters of heretics, in various ways; but, wishing to act with benevolence, and in order that your souls may not be lost, since our Lord does not wish the death of the sinner but his reformation and life; by these presents, we remove and suspend the censure promulgated by the said former inquisitors against you, so long as you observe and comply with the terms of this our edict, by which we require, exhort and order you, in virtue of the holy obedi-ence, and under penalty of complete excommunication, within nine days from the time that the present edict shall have been read to you, or made known to you in whatsoever manner, to state all that you know, have seen, heard, or heard tell in any manner whatsoever, of the things and ceremonies above-men-tioned, and to appear before us personally to declare and mani-fest what you have seen, heard, or heard tell secretly, without having spoken previously with any other person, or borne false witness against anyone. Otherwise, the period having passed, the canonical admonitions having been repeated in accordance with the law, steps will be taken to give out and promulgate sentence of excommunication against you, in and by these docu-

ments; and through such excommunication, we order that you
be publicly denounced; and if, after a further period of nine
days, you should persist in your rebellion and excommunication,
you shall be excommunicated, anathematised, cursed, segregated,
and separated as an associate of the devil, from union with and
inclusion in the holy Mother-Church, and the sacraments of the
same. And we order the vicars, rectors, chaplains, and sacristans
and any other religious or ecclesiastical persons to regard and
treat the above-mentioned as excommunicated and accursed
for having incurred the wrath and indignation of Almighty
God, and of the glorious Virgin Mary, His Mother, and of the
beatified apostles Saint Peter and Saint Paul, and all the saints of
the celestial Court; and upon such rebels and disobedient ones
who would hide the truth regarding the above-mentioned things,
be all the plagues and maledictions which befell and descended
upon King Pharaoh and his host for not having obeyed the
divine commandments; and the same sentence of divine excommunication encompass them as it encompassed the people of
Sodom and Gomorrah who all perished in flames; and of Athan
and Abiron who were swallowed up into the earth for the
great delinquencies and sins which they committed in dis-
obedience and rebellion against our Lord God; and may they
be accursed in eating and drinking, in waking and sleeping, in
coming and going. Accursed be they in living and dying, and
may they ever be hardened to their sins, and the devil be at
their right hand always; may their vocation be sinful, and their
days be few and evil; may their substance be enjoyed by
others, and their children be orphans, and their wives widows.
May their children ever be in need, and may none help them;
may they be turned out of their homes and their goods taken
by usurers; and may they find nobody to have compassion on
them; may their children be ruined and outcast, and their
names also; and their wickedness be ever present in the divine
memory. May their enemies vanquish them and despoil them of
all they possess in the world; and may they wander from door
to door without relief. May their prayers be turned to maledictions; and accursed be the bread and wine, the meat and fish,
the fruit and other food that they eat; likewise the houses they
inhabit and the raiment they wear, the beasts upon which they

ride and the beds upon which they sleep, and the tables and the napkins upon which they eat. Accursed be they to Satan and to Lucifer and to all the devils in hell, and these be their lords, and accompany them by night and day. Amen. And if any persons incurring the said excommunications and maledictions, should persist therein for the space of a year, they should be regarded as heretics themselves, and shall be prosecuted by the same process as against heretics or suspects of the crime of heresy. Given on the   March, in the year of our Lord God, one thousand five hundred and twelve."

(Item: Of no avail is the confession made to the confessor for procuring absolution from the sentence of excommunication to which the heretic might be subject, from the time the crime was committed.)

(Item: All who know anything of the things mentioned in this present edict, or of other heresies, and do not come forward to denounce and declare the same, are hereby excommunicated and may not be absolved by their confessors.)

El doctor
Palacio, inquisidor."

10 *Yitzhak Fritz Baer*
Jewish and Converso Trials

Y. F. Baer does, in these selections about the Inquisition's investigations of Jews and Marranos, what Schäfer did for the tribunal and the Protestants: he presents the raw data to us for our digestion and interpretation. The continuing situation emerging from his evidence involved far greater numbers of persons; it also revealed the tremendous and tragic pressures under which Jews and Marranos alike labored. Many of the latter clearly were hounded by some sort of "ancestral guilt," even where the original apostasy had been several generations earlier. Many Jews, prior, of course, to the expulsion of all professing Jews in 1492, were torn between envy of the Marranos' escape from their own increasingly precarious situation, which, how-

*ever, was marked by equally growing "Old Christian" hostility to-
ward the converts, and pride in their religious steadfastness, however
occasionally self-defeating that might be. Equally, numbers of "New
Christians" resented the remaining Jews as many became increasingly
sincere and devout Catholics, whereas some Jews, at least, thought
unrealistically—and dangerously—in terms of reclaiming the apostates
to the old faith. The mysticism and hysteria on the part of some of
the latter could not go unnoticed by the Inquisition, which tended
to overgeneralize about various Jewish communities from the words
and acts of handfuls of people. From the Catholic viewpoint, there was
enough relapsing into Judaizing practices by Marranos to warrant the
"final solution" of 1492, which, as the evidence from Baer and Roth
strongly suggests, was a most incomplete and tension-producing act.
Finally, in tandem with Schäfer's materials, one notes from Baer the
success of the Inquisition (indeed, of society itself in general) in
playing off the various accused and witnesses against one another; in
this the law of silence affecting all inquisitorial proceedings was of
fundamental significance.*

P. 450. April 30, 1492. Statement of Rabbi Levi aben Sento
of Zaragoza who had preached in the synagogue about the ban
on speaking on the Inquisition and the expulsion edict of April
29.

". . . about two years ago at the inquisitors' behest I gave
three sermons on three successive Saturdays . . . exhorting the
Jews to tell all they knew about Christians who were judaizing
or engaging in heretical practices [saying that] the inquisitors
would pardon them if they did thusly . . . ." [Since technically
the Holy Office was not supposed to have authority over unconverted Jews this brief statement speaks volumes about the
Jewish communities' precarious situation in the last years up to
the expulsion. Ed.]

Pp. 468-472. February-August, 1468. The Toleda-Cordoba

SOURCE. Yitzhak Fritz Baer, *Die Juden In Christlichen Spanion* (Berlin:
Shocken Verlag, 1936), I, ii, pp. 450, 468–476, 478–79, 479–483, 484–500, 512–
515, and 519–528. Reprinted by permission of publisher and author.

process against the converso Master [a Commander] of the
Order of Santiago, Juan de Pineda. From the *accusatio:* Pineda
"heretic . . . denying the advent of our savior and redeemer,
Jesus Christ, desiring the Turk to be the Messiah [in terms of
saving Spanish Jewry], wishing others to glorify the Mosaic
law and that Judaism should have good Jews and prophets saved
by the Mosaic Law alone. [He also thought] that the conversos
living near Villa Real . . . where there were many Christians,
were mistaken and not aware of what they were doing . . . [and
should have known] that the Turk would be the destroyer of
Christianity and protector of Judaism . . . ."
    . . . Pineda's statements in his self-defence.
"Item . . . Negotiations of great importance were confided in
me during the reign of Henry IV [of Castile, 1454-1474] . . .
with Alfonso Carillo, Archbishop of Toledo and Don Juan de
Pacheco [I went on a mission] to Pope Sixtus IV . . . where
he made count of the sacred palace and nuncio (?) in the place
he was sending me . . . [I] always wrote as a Christian, enemy
of the Turks [and rejoiced at] news of Christian victories . . .
[he suggests that the jealousy and envy of others is behind his
present troubles, particularly concerning his favor from Rome
and a dispute over one of his estates] . . . I have always believed in . . . Christ . . . detesting the sect of Turks and Moors
. . . I never praised the Mosaic Law nor said that Christian
conversos were wrong for being good Christians . . . the Turks
would oppress Jews more than Christians . . . I never said that
the Turks would come to Castile [disposed towards?] the
conversos. . . ."
    [The witness Juan de Estrada, a canon of the largest church
in Toledo certified the correctness of Pineda's remarks about
his mission to Rome; several others also verified this.]
    Juan del Rio, prebend of Toledo testified to having heard
"Rodrigo de Jaen, canon of Seville . . . Pineda's cousin, . . . say
that the Commander [Pineda] was always a good Christian [but]
I heard this witness tell Pedro de Vergara, prebend, when the
Commander was arrested, that he was a heretic . . . [implies
Pineda was a bigamist, too] . . . . About four years ago when
a Portuguese armada arrived in Rome en route to fight the

Turks [Baer notes this was in 1481] Pineda joined it with some Italians . . . and when any good news about Christian successes arrived he was pleased. . . ."

Diego de Ayala, inhabitant of Toledo, testified to having ". . . heard from Alfonso Acafra, who had been the Commander's tailor in Cordoba, that during the plunder of the conversos [there in 1473] Pineda had said that the Turk was the glorifier [savior?] of the Mosaic Law. . . ."

Pedro de Casaruyos of Toledo claimed that another Cordoba tailor, Juan de Baena, had said that Pineda told him: "You don't know who the Turk is. If God has made [him] for us . . . then this one is the destroyer of Christendom and defender of Judaism and is the Messiah promised in Jewish law."

A Friar Miguel of the monastery of San Bernaldo accused Pineda of having said ". . . some twelve-thirteen years before . . . that in Judea there were good Jews who were saved in their law and prophets [, not by] the death of . . . Christ. . . ."

Casaruyos added in a second appearance that Pineda had been involved with "a hosier of Cordoba, Juan de Madrid, in order to observe certain Mosaic ceremonies. [Madrid] was taken as a heretic to the Bishop's jail where . . . he said that the Mosaic Law was good . . . the people stoned him and after a day the Commander and one of his brothers [who had an important position in the Jewish quarter; this seems to mean a brother of the hosier's] . . . said how they had stoned [him, too; but actually they had prayed for his soul according to the witness] . . . Pineda was considered a converso . . . who was there to fight the Old Christians of Cordoba alongside the conversos. . . .

"Pineda was relaxed on August 16, 1486."

Pp. 473-476. Process of Friar Alfonso de Toledo, monk of Sisla de Toledo. November 27, 1487-July 28, 1488. Judaizer. Planned to flee the country to escape the Inquisition. Accused of calling burnt conversos martyrs. Testimony of Mose Hadida of Toledo. ". . . Eight years before while . . . at the monastery of Sisla to see his brother Ysaque [Isaac] Hadida who worked there . . . he had heard it said of . . . Alfonso . . . that he fasted on Yom Kippur which [he claimed] was the best fast day and that he observed the [Jewish] Sabbath. . . ."

Testimony of Samuel Valenci, Jew of Toledo. ". . . two

years before . . . he spoke with . . . Alfonso . . . at . . . Sisla secretly . . . [who] told this witness that his wish was to serve God and withdraw from this monastery . . . [Alfonso then informed Valenci they were kinsmen] . . . the friar related his life story to [Valenci and] how twice he had left the Order intending to go abroad and how he had returned . . . to do penance [for this] . . . but back at Sisla he found . . . he could not in good conscience pray, etc. . . . [Alfonso's plea for Valenci's help and shelter was refused]. . . . Another day this witness [conversed with the accused] . . . who asked not to be called Friar Alfonso any longer but . . . Jacob . . . [adding that] he had now passed from the shadow to God's service." [This particular testimony vividly portrays the mental anguish of many conversos, especially those who, in all likely initial sincerity, entered the clergy, but whose subsequent development led them down this dangerous path. Ed.]

. . . Several of his fellow monks charged him with expressing sympathy for executed "martyrs," whom he was said to view as thereby "saved." At the news that the Inquisition was investigating the Order "Friar Alfonso walked as one very upset and as a dead man." He compared burnt conversos to "the martyred Maccabees, saying they were most glorious and excellent men who had died for the Mosaic Law."

One of the witnesses declared that he had heard from his father "that Friar Alfonso's father was Jewish and had turned Christian, but had been able to read only Hebrew." Another said that "when the Inquisition came to Toledo . . . Alfonso became a fugitive; that his brother, a secular priest, was [also] in great fear of the Inquisition." A monk observed that the accused "had fled the monastery three times and returned each time and had heard him express a desire to become a Franciscan (?)."

[Alfonso claimed to have been misunderstood concerning his statements which led to a search for more witnesses, who supported the previously given evidence of his Judaizing. This section of the record was lost. The accused was purged and then absolved, which implies some favorable testimony must have been forthcoming.]

Pp. 478-479. Process of Aldonza Gonzalez, wife of Fernando

de Jaen, of San Martin de Valdeiglesias. July 15, 1486—Relaxed July 25, 1488. Kept from her youth a Jewish prayerbook. Prayed in a synagogue, and allowed Jews to pray for her husband's welfare. Concealed the prayerbook with a Jewess.

From her confession of July 15, 1486. ". . . when I was a girl in my father's house twenty years ago . . . a Rabbi David . . . [of] Segovia who came and left [at will; freely] in his house . . . showed me how to read [Hebrew, apparently] . . . [I showed the Jewish prayerbook] to my abbot uncle . . . who said it was against our holy Catholic faith and that I should destroy it . . . sometimes I went to synagogue with one of the Duchess' (?) daughters and other duennas of the town . . . ." [The prosecutor notes at this point that during the plague the accused wore a Jewish amulet. . . . A townsman claims that she attended both Christian and Hebrew services, and recalled her temporary excommunication, then reconciliation with the local church. Two Rabbis testify that five and fifteen years earlier, respectively, she had come to them at synagogue, mainly to pray for her husband's success in various activities.]

Rica, wife of Jaco aben Rocas, said that "eight or nine years before while doing the accused's wash . . . [the latter] told her that she fasted on some of the Jewish fast days . . . and six or seven years ago . . . Aldonza had told [her] at her house, with great anxiety, about a friar who had preached in the town, and she had begged [Rica] to hold a book for her . . . [for awhile] . . . she showed it to her husband and he ordered her . . . to return it . . . although she did not know what the book was about . . . when she did, Aldonza implored her never to speak about [this episode]. . . ."

Pp. 479-483. Summary of process of Mencia Suares, beata [mystic laywoman] of Ocaña [a center of occasionally heterodox mystical practices] in Toledo, August 20, 1487—February 28, 1490. Sentenced to abjuration de vehementi and penance. Accused of skeptical remarks about Christianity and favorable ones about Judaism as a religion; not specifically charged with observing Jewish rites, however [i.e. Judaizing]. . . .

Two witnesses accused her of saying prayers revolving about the Old Testament figures of Joseph and Joshua and a prayerbook was taken from her containing the Hebrew word, *Adonai*

[God, Lord] several times, but which otherwise read like a "typical mystical effusion," ending with an invocation of Jesus Christ. [This book also had references to Hebrew words such as *Sion* and *Israel*, once each.]

Pp. 512-515. Process of Fernando de Madrid, deceased, of Torrelaguna. September 13, 1491-1492. Expressed messianic hopes and prophesies concerning the Spanish government's regulations against the Jews.

Isaac Alfandari, Jew of Torrelaguna, spent much time with the accused who ". . . prayed to God . . . to deliver us from this people under whose eyes we are and with whom we must live dishonestly. . . ."

Isaac de Bilhorado of Torrelaguna said ". . . about ten years ago . . . saw [the accused] . . . many times at his father's house where [they] prayed and studied the [Hebrew] prophets . . . and [the accused] said . . . there would be no betterment until . . . the Messiah came . . . [spoke of revenge on the persecutors]. . . ."

Jaco de Bilhorado, butcher of Torrelaguna said "Fernando de Madrid . . . believed the Jewish law superior to the Christian one . . . [they discussed the Messiah's coming many times] . . . he told [the witness] that the Messiah could not come until the conversos had paid for having turned Christian, and one day, he showed a paper to him on which were some Hebrew letters which the witness could not read . . . [Madrid] said a wise Jew had given this to him. . . ."

Alfonso de Marino, son of Ferrand Martines, cooper, said ". . . twelve years ago . . . Madrid said that had the Antichrist appeared in the city of blows that is Seville (*Note*. The first great anti-Semitic riot in Spain was there in 1391. Ed.) . . . he would sell his properties and go to live with him." Judgment: condemnation.

Pp. 484-500. Collective trials in Huesca because of communal circumcising of Christians and hindering of Jews wishing to convert. January 10, 1489-June 14, 1490.

Statement of Master Acach Rondi, who with other Jews, prevented the conversion of Rabbi Eliazar Alitienca "four or five years ago [we: names several] . . . swore by the truth of an agreement written in Hebrew [this appears to have been

a compact binding the Huesca Jews to fight conversion in their
ranks]. . . . The other Jews . . . [read this] to Alitienca . . .
for whose sake the agreement had been composed . . . these
two (?) depositions the Jews ordered made public . . . [by]
Rabbi Juceu Papui.

"Asked what was in the [compact, Rondi] said he thought
besides having written of Jesus as a non-Christian (?) . . .
Eliezar swore to God and by the Holy Father's life and by the
King and Queen to become Christian in a certain time . . . It
seemed to Alitienca [and another Rabbi's son] that Christ's law
was superior to his and they agreed to convert . . . [but this leaked
out to the Huesca Jews and he was ostracized by all, his father and
uncles included in order to dissuade him from converting]. . . ."

Statement of Abram Almosino. March 11. ". . . there arrived
Johan de Ciudat [original spelling, suggesting naturalization.
Ed.] [who had spent time in Valencia with a 'wise' Jewish
Rabbi] . . . [Ciudat] had gone to Constantinople to convert
to Judaism and . . . Bivagch and brought him to his house . . .
Ciudat expressed his wish to be circumcised . . . very secretly
. . . [Later, as the witness] was leaving synagogue Master
Abram . . . called ten or twelve of the most important Jews
. . . and all went to his house [to confer with Ciudat about
the foregoing] . . . Ciudat left with Abram and I never saw
him again . . . this was some twenty-five years ago."

On May 13th this witness added that "Five or six days after
this meeting at Bivagch's house, Ciudat returned there and was
circumcised in presence of several." [Under subsequent torture
Almosino later gave more names in connection with this ceremony.]

Other witnesses indicated various Rabbis performed circum-
cisions and one testified that "a Samuel Parenti, Portuguese
. . . Christian lived in the *Judería* (Jewish quarter. Ed.)
teaching himself how to be a Jew. . . ." This was followed by
a statement from the Jewish Council of Huesca promising to
reject any future would-be converts to Judaism. An edict to this
effect from the Inquisition to be posted in the synagogue
followed the text.

March 11, 1489. Testimony of the accused, Haym Fischl.
"About thirty years ago Master Abram Bivagch told [me] that

a Castilian named Johan de Ciudat had come here and confessed that while passing through Jerusalem he had converted to Judaism . . . . On April 2 Fischl was subject to formal denunciation for having lied [by virtue of] Almosino's testimony of March 13 [which had specifically named him; obviously Fischl tried to shift the 'guilt' for Ciudat's Judaism away from his community]." Further testimony from others along these lines. [Baer points out on page 495 that in these specific types of cases jurisdiction was technically royal, not inquisitorial; presumably because it involved professing, unconverted Jews. Ed.]

From further evidence of Jewish perjuries, etc., at Huesca. "Master Acach Vivag . . . converted by the Holy Spirit to Christ's faith, received Baptism . . . swore in the presence of many worthies to discharge his soul of danger that he had deposed falsely . . . against [various names ensue] Jews [now] imprisoned by the Inquisition. . . ." [This appears to suggest Vivag had been a spy against his brethren before conversion. Ed.]

From Baer's introduction to the next section. "The Fiscal [prosecutor for the Inquisition] touched on the cases of Solomon Arama and Juce Cardador whom [Abram] Alitienca had led back to Judaism . . . [and he remarked further] about the Jews mania for converts and on the worthlessness of the witnesses defending them.

". . . Abram Alitienca, fearing neither our God nor this Holy Office, nor [the laws of the state] has long dared to induce, pervert, circumcise, and convert . . . Jewish Christians, heretics, apostates, and others to many nefarious abominations against the holy Catholic faith and our redeemer, Jesus Christ, to the damnation and perdition of many Christian souls [while upholding the Jewish law and faith to other Jews who were prevented from converting]. . . . [This] Jew . . . perverted Christians to the Jewish law and had them make grand obeisance [to Christian laws] while apostasizing in order to save their properties, etc. . . [the Fiscal then cites earlier Jewish writings presumably justifying such behavior] . . . always such Jews were liars, false, deceiving prophets . . . of the people, as in Jeremiah, chapters XXII and XXVIII [!], because by their malice and enmity against Christians their testimonies ought not to be admitted

. . . no Jew can swear truly against another . . . [as they will all aid one another], especially in cases like these inasmuch as they believe that to save another Jew is a good and holy venture, while to have subverted Christians to his damned law [is viewed as a great achievement] . . . [there follows a lengthy defence by one of the accused, Alitienca apparently, rejecting much of the adverse testimony, and refuting the Fiscal's efforts to relate 'dechristianizing' of converts to Hebrew precepts, especially concerning the giving of false witness, etc.] [The entire transcript strongly indicates the most confused psychology and religious torment of both accusers and witnesses. Considering how this process had commenced it is curious that Eliazar Alitienca's brother apparently ended up among the accused. Ed.] All relaxed on June 14, 1490."

Pp. 519-528. Process of *Licenciado* [lawyer, in local government] Diego de Alva of Cuellar, at Avila. Favored Jews. Through his care the Jewish community at Cuellar grew from 50 to 200 persons. He afforded a Jewish student admission to the town secretly with respect to the [Jewish] Sabbath. Helped prevent [or hinder] the baptism of Jewish children. Attended synagogue to hear a Rabbi preach on Rosh Hashonah, the Jewish New Year's. Equivocal in his official treatment of Jews . . . Many Jews had sworn to denounce the Conversos because the expulsion was their fault. . . .

Testimony of Mose Poco, Jew of Cuellar, shoemaker, confirmed by Mose Abenvenir, now Francisco Sanchez since his baptism, reflecting on an incident in 1488 concerning the conversion of Rabbi [and physician] Samuel, now called Master Fabricio, "that the Rabbi's sermons in synagogue were attended by many Christians, Conversos and Old, . . . among whom was Doña Leonor, the Duke of Albuquerque's aunt and many [other persons from the upper classes]. . . ."

Referring to the year 1490 the Franciscan monk, Francisco de Villahe [Baer is uncertain of this spelling] testified against Alva, saying that he favored Jews in his legal capacities, quoting the "Babylonian Talmud" against Christian writings, calling the former "our law. . . ." This witness made the claim that Alva was instrumental in enlarging the Cuellar Jewish community.

Elsewhere in this process Alva was designated as an *alguacil*
and *alcalde* for the Duke of Albuquerque [who presumably
held Cuellar under his senioral authority; *alguacil*—principal
local police officer, *alcalde*—local judicial figure. Ed.] Other
witnesses noted Alva's regard for the Jewish Sabbath and his
marriage to Jewess who brought him a handsome dowry; also
reiterated his synagogue attendance [which his marriage might
explain. Ed.]

Friar Pedro de Castro de Ordiales, a Franciscan, testified on
March 14, 1498 that some twenty years previously the newly
converted Master Fabricio (see above) had told him of his
earlier preachings at synagogue in Cuellar which had lured many
Christians, among them the accused. This had caused "great
scandal in Cuellar, especially in the monastery of San Francisco
[Ordiales's own] and Friar Francisco de Espinosa, then head of
the cloister, preached against this, as did this witness. Because
of [our efforts] people ceased listening to [Fabricio, then Rabbi
Samuel]. . . ."

Gomez de Rojas, *regidor* [one of the principal municipal
officials] of Cuellar, April 3, 1498. "Twenty-five years ago . . .
Old Christians and Conversos went to hear his [Fabricio's]
sermons . . . including the lawyer Alva, *alcalde* . . . [who,]
said he went to hear Samuel preach on great matters of philosophy, grammar, and other things . . . [Alva accused of being
intimate with the heretical (Judaizing) head of the monastery
of San Francisco de Avila, staying with him in his cell many
times, not seeing anyone else]." Alva was acquitted. Some of
the witnesses were found to be liars and personal enemies.
Rabbi Samuel—Master Fabricio was called "a very bad person
and was a great usurer who held [Alva] in great enmity for
many reasons . . . [such as bringing him to justice and causing
him to lose some of his usurious gains]. . . ."

11   *Ernst Schäfer*
                             Protestants' Trials

*Ernst Schäfer was, for all practical purposes, the German equivalent
of Lea, with one important exception. In his scrupulous compilation
of most of the extant sources concerning the trials and executions of
the handful of Spanish Protestants, real or imagined, in mid-sixteenth
century, he seems to have avoided making judgments. Schäfer was
content to prepare the primary data in usable form, and let scholarly
readers draw their own conclusions. Undoubtedly for that reason,
Spanish historians have not felt the need to take up the cudgels with
him as many still do today with Lea. Yet, as these selections graph-
ically illustrate, the operations of the Inquisition, sustained from above
and below in lay society, could be fully as awesome as Llorente and
Lea claimed. The testimony of the past laid before us by Schäfer is
a compelling case of undifferentiated fear of and hostility to dissent,
as well as outright heresy; the diminutiveness of the number of the
accused obviously was irrelevant at the time, as was the precise character of their religious thought, which apparently ranged from some
kind of vague but outright Protestantism to the fringes of "liberal"
Catholicism. It is very necessary to bear in mind, however, in reading
this sort of material, that the Protestant and other Catholic countries
of the day were hardly more accommodating in many respects to
heterodoxy in its varied forms. Toleration in different degrees frequently was the result of governmental weakness, not strength; it was
rarely granted or observed from conviction, but from expediency.*

Pp. 405-410, *Accusatio* from the Valladolid Inquisition in
1559 against Marina de Guevara, who followed "the perverse
and condemned heresiarch Luther and other heretics. . . ."

SOURCE. Ernst Schafer, *Beitrage zur Geschichte des Spanischen Protes-
tantismus und die Inquisition* (Gutersloh: C. Bertelsmann Verlag, 1902),
Vol. 1, pp. 405-410, 428-430, 433-435, 440-441, 443-446, and 449-452.

1. Established her original baptism and that she was a nun in the nearby monastery of Belem of the Order of St. Bernard.

2. She believed that "faith without works justified believers saying that through Christ's passion and merits all sinners were justified . . . according [to] the section on justification held by the Lutheran heretics. . . .

3. In the presence of others she said that to achieve heaven it was not necessary to do works and believed that those works of penance, fasting, and prayer were not needed for men's salvation and justification."

4. She "believed and communicated this to others that in the hereafter there was no purgatory for the souls of the departed."

5. She believed and also communicated to others that "Papal pronouncements [bulls, etc.] . . . were profitless . . . and held no worth concerning the remission and pardoning of sins."

6. And that "sacrifices, masses, offerings, and other aids one made and offered in the Catholic Church for souls in purgatory were useless and relieved the defunct of nothing."

7. And that "in the Catholic Church there should be no more than three sacraments, that is, baptism, penance, and communion, for the other sacraments used and administered by the Holy Mother Church are not sacraments and have no efficacy." [Note inclusion of penance and respectful reference to the "Holy Mother Church" suggesting the nun was doubtless not a Protestant; more likely a Valdesian type. Ed.][1]

8. She, with others, "performed the Eucharist with bread and wine . . . without confessing [i.e., according to the Lutheran custom]. . . ."

9. She believed that "the Holy Mother Apostolic Catholic Church of Rome does not govern nor is governed by the Holy Spirit. . ."

. . . 13. She "owned and read certain books and handwritten manuscripts containing many Lutheran errors which others also read. . . ."

14. She "wrote and received many letters and notices in

---

[1] Valdesian—followers of Juan Valdés (about 1500–1541), an influential Spanish Catholic thinker of heterodox views, some of whose Italian followers ended up as Protestants.

which . . . she and the others were fortified in their sect and errors."

15. Accused of being in touch with the Seville heretics, and of trying to hide matters from the Inquisition while also advising others to act similarly.

16-18. Accused of calling "brothers" persons who were Lutherans whom she called "true Christians," taken by the Inquisition as believers in this sect. [Guilt by association, too. Ed.]

. . . 21. She "affirmed that Christians were Pharisees and 'ceremonialists' who did not understand and believe in this sect and its errors. . . .

. . . 24. Thus Marina de Guevara has committed . . . heresy and apostasy . . . against our Holy Catholic faith and Christian religion . . . the accused [is] an apostate, heretical Lutheran . . . [deserving] the extreme penalties . . . of the Holy Office [i.e., relaxation] . . . [further torture is advised to make her reveal what is presumed more information about others like herself]. . . ."

Pp. 428-430. Torture of a Savoyard, Miguel Barambun, in Toledo in 1587.

After preliminary inquiry, including torture and vacillation on the accused's part, he said "He was a Lutheran in La Rochelle [Huguenot fortified seaport in west France] and has received the holy sacrament thrice in all his life [seems to refer to the Mass and/or Eucharist]. . . .

INQUISITOR: What things did he do as a Lutheran in La-Rochelle?

ACCUSED: "[We] robbed [Catholics] for gains."

. . . INQUISITOR: Requested him to give particulars of his heretical beliefs.

ACCUSED: Among other things he denied the Papacy's authority, the Mass, the prohibition on meat, and in answer to a repetition of this question said that he "believed he'd saved his life by being Lutheran and then warned to speak the truth said he'd been a Lutheran without knowing what he was saying. [Furthermore] he hadn't believed in God because of his disbelief in the Mass and its priests when they performed this ritual . . . [therefore it was] better to be a Lutheran than disbelieve in the Mass. . . ."

INQUISITOR: *What did the Lutherans say about the Mass?*

ACCUSED: "Not good, not sacerdotal, because the poor people cannot eat [partake of the bread and wine with the clergy] . . . ."

INQUISITOR: Threatens further torture if the truth be not forthcoming. . . .

ACCUSED: The Lutherans "don't believe in the Mass, or in the saints . . . the torture made him restore in his heart [these beliefs] ". . . [Later says that he] "has been Lutheran all my life . . . but the torture . . . [was reconverting him to Catholicism]." [The torture lasted about ten hours, according to Schäfer; the outcome of this process is not known. Ed.]

Pp. 433-435. Sentencing of Pedro de Cazalla for Lutheranism in 1559 by the Valladolid tribunal.

The accused ". . . having confessed to us that for four years he had communicated with a certain person who had been his friend for fourteen years and who had instructed him in [the Lutheran explanation] of justification . . . [this friend] had suggested to him that there was no need to stop at the denial of purgatory, and from this inferred the uselessness of indulgences and things conceded by the Pope. . . . [It was pointed out that] Pedro de Cazalla was descended from converted Jews on both sides . . . [and had] instructed and indoctrinated many others about the passion and merits of our redeemer, Jesus Christ, who had justified all sinners without recourse to works, penance. . . .

"Item . . . Cazalla believed in faith alone without works . . . penance, fasts, prayers . . . [none of the latter being] meritorious nor profitable for sinner's salvation, saying they were only justified by Christ's passion and merits.

"Item . . . believed there was no purgatory in the next life . . . and held the same error about the sacrifices, offerings, prayers, and aids in the Catholic Church for the deceased . . . [considering] all such aids superfluous and without effect.

"Item . . . believed that Christians who had faith did not have to have recourse to the saints, saying that the saints' intercession

. . . had no effect concerning the salvation of sinners.

"Item . . . believed that the Apostolic Roman Catholic Church had no power or authority to force any Christians to observe its precepts, fast, vigils, celebrations, nor prohibit or make [special] distinctions about foods.

"Item, [he asserted] that the Pope or other eminence . . . had no power to excommunicate or absolve any Christian by means of indulgences, jubilees, and pardons . . . which were worthless . . . concerning the pardoning of sins.

"Item, [he denounced monasticism].

"Item . . . believed that oral confession . . . is not necessary, nor is a sacrament, nor is useful for the pardon and absolution of sins . . . [instead Cazalla recommended a kind of mental confession to God, directly and alone].

"Item . . . believed that the Catholic Church should have no more than two sacraments (cf. the nun Guevara, from the same group), baptism and communion in memory of the passion and [last] supper of the savior while the others . . . were not sacraments [this seems to be a quasi-Zwinglian view of the Eucharist, which testified to the book-smugglers' diligence in getting other than Lutheran Protestant works into Spain. Ed.]
. . . .

"Item . . . believed that the . . . Eucharist of the consecrated host and chalice is not . . . Christ . . . nor sacramental, but only spiritual through the faith of the recipient and [He is] not really or corporeally [present] as our Holy Catholic faith and mother church has taught us. [This probably can be interpreted in several Protestant ways. Ed.]

"Item . . . believed that all Christians, priests and laymen, could administer and receive the . . . Eucharist under both kinds, of bread and of wine. . . . [Classic statement of priesthood of all believers. Ed.]

"Item . . . Cazalla had made communion . . . with many others . . . according to the Lutheran usage . . . many times in diverse places, while hearing and preaching before this supper a sermon about the sect and errors of Luther in which [Lutheranism] was praised as the truth.

". . . Item, in Cazalla's house were such [heretical] meetings held and . . . [he owned and loaned out] the heretical books of Luther and Calvin, and many other heretics.

"Item . . . declaring our definitive sentence that he is an apostate heretical Lutheran [Cazalla is sentenced to relaxation, confiscation of all goods, etc.]. . . ."

Pp. 440-441. Sentence of Julián Hernández in 1560 by the Seville tribunal. The accused named a deacon of the Lutheran Walloon Church of Frankfurt [which was true, although he appears to have been gravitating toward Calvinism near his life's end; cf. J.E. Longhurst, "Julián Hernández," *BHR*[2] art. Ed.].

He "had brought many [heretical] books [to Seville] . . . and so accepting his confession . . . we declare him to be a pertinacious Lutheran abettor and concealer of heretics [sentence of relaxation and confiscation of goods follows]. . . . [From other witnesses we know that he] had gone to Paris about eight or nine years before and from there traveled to Scotland and Germany . . . and came to Seville to disseminate . . . Lutheran literature and get in touch with persons desiring also to go to Germany to live with the Lutherans . . . [and subvert true Catholics]. . . ."

[Hernández appears to have been the only Spanish Reformation heretic to visit Scotland, if this account is fully accurate, and that would have probably been prior to the triumph of Knox and Calvinism. Ed.]

Pp. 443-446. *Auto de fe* at Valladolid, May 21, 1559, attended by Don Carlos and the Regent, Princess Juana, Philip II's son and sister respectively; the King had not yet returned from the Netherlands.

"This *auto* was held in the Plaza de San Francisco on a very large platform [there follows a very minute, detailed description of local arrangements for the occasion and the social eminence of the onlookers, including high clergy as well as laymen] . . . before the *auto* began a letter from the Holy Office was read imploring the princes [Carlos and Juana] and others . . . to aid the Inquisition [and the true faith generally] to punish and extirpate all errors, heresy, and apostacy . . . and Don Carlos and Princess

[2] *BHR: Bibliothèque d'Humanisme et Renaissance*, XXII (1960), 90-118.

Juana swore [to do as much] on the Gospels and the Cross . . . which all received with great admiration, joy, and contentment. Friar Melchor de Cano [the noted Dominican supporter of the tribunal and the ongoing scholastic revival of Thomism in Spain. Ed.] began to read the sentences in a very impressive manner . . . [fifteen burnt, sixteen reconciled]. . . ." "Continuation of this *auto*, pp. 449-452. "Agustin de Cazalla, Francisco de Vivero, and Alonso de Pérez [to be burnt] passed by the Princes' platform to the heretics'. The Bishop of Palencia and the grandly apparelled pontifical representative . . . formally degraded [unfrocked] these three clerics.

". . . Cazalla, at this, gave great indications of contrition with tears before all; . . . Vivero was smiling while Pérez displayed no feelings at the moment of this humiliation. Cazalla went down on his knees before the Princes saying in tears [he pleaded for his several relations arrested and sentenced with him, especially for an aged sister; otherwise he seemed to collapse pathetically] . . . [the executions start] Cazalla [, hysterical], proclaiming his belief in the Holy Mother Church of Rome for which he is dying . . . Vivero, Pérez, and Antonio Herrezuelo silent . . . Cazalla in a great voice said he died for having been Lutheran . . . but was repenting . . . and all those dying with him were dying for his doctrine, and by his inducement and great sympathy persuaded Herrezuelo to convert to Christ's faith [i.e., Cazalla's repudiation of his "Lutheranism" drove the latter to also deny it and revert to Catholicism; Herrezuelo subsequently went back on this recantation]. . . . The others did not show any feelings or demonstrate repentance . . . and thus were burnt alive. . . .

"Tuesday, the next day, dawn came to the Plaza and the scaffold. . . ."

12   *John E. Longhurst*
The Process of an Erasmian Charged with Lutheranism

John E. Longhurst's monograph on the Uceda process has the merit of enabling the reader to follow in considerable detail the unfolding of an individual but complete inquisitorial proceeding, from the accusation which commenced the investigations through the final judgment. Diego de Uceda's trial, some thirty years before the Seville and Valladolid mass agonies described by Schäfer, foreshadows much of the latter. Uceda, of course, got off much more leniently, but the attitudes on the part of clergy and laity alike in the course of his travails, were quite similar to those revealed by approximately 1560. Indeed, one is impressed not so much by any meaningful differences between the late 1520's and late 1550's as by the hardening and intensification of earlier views toward heterodoxy. The Uceda trial suggests very strongly that Philip II alone was hardly responsible, as is often assumed, for the growing rigidity of Spanish attitudes in this and similar matters. Their elements were already on hand, which is, however, not to deny that most of Europe underwent from mid-sixteenth century a freezing of attitudes into more orthodox and rigid channels regarding the faintest hint of religious (and political) deviation. If some of the victims of the autos-de-fe in the Schäfer documents seem not to have been any kind of genuine Protestant (although clearly some were), the more or less Erasmian[1] Uceda who emerges from Longhurst's careful account most assuredly was not a "Lutheran." It is equally important to be aware, as this case surely shows, that not only did the Inquisition move frequently with agonizing slowness, but that by contemporary standards, it also deliberated very carefully and even fairly. Its major shortcomings, from our vantage point, have been observed in the selections from Lynch and Elliott. Furthermore,

---

[1] Very broadly, Erasmian Catholicism (about 1500–1530) stressed following Jesus Christ as a great moral—ethical example, without, however challenging doctrinal orthodoxy, the sacraments, etc. It also tended to attack contemporary church abuses. See Introduction for extended comment.

as the Uceda process reveals, an investigation, however lengthy, cer-
tainly did not always conclude with a severe sentence. No doubt, the
result here probably was, on the whole, socially and psychologically
harmful, which is not to be underestimated in sixteenth century
Castile.

On Saturday, January 25, 1528, Diego de Uceda left the Emperor's court at Burgos for Córdoba. During the twenty-four
days of his journey he made three overnight stops of more than
ordinary importance:

(1) Cerezo: January 30, 1528

At the local inn, where he stayed overnight, Diego conversed
with one Rodrigo Durán who, with his servant Juan de Avellaneda, was on his way to Seville to embark for the New World.

(2) Guadarrama: February 14, 1528

Here he spoke with García Alvarez, archpriest of Arjona,and
Cristóbal Juárez, a canon from León. The following morning
Diego left Guadarrama with the archpriest and the canon. The
three lunched together at Bailén, where the canon left the others.
Diego and the archpriest continued together to Arjona where
Diego spent the night at the archpriest's home.

(3) Baena: February 16, 1528

At the local inn Diego spoke with the landlady and an uniden-
tified old lady.

Two days later, February 18, 1528, Diego de Uceda arrived
in Córdoba.

Toledo: February 11, 1528

On this date one Rodrigo Durán voluntarily appeared before
the Holy Office of the Inquisition of Toledo to make a state-

SOURCE. John E. Longhurst, *Luther And The Spanish Inquisition: The
Case Of Diego de Uceda, 1528–1529* (Albuquerque: University of New
Mexico Press, 1953), pp. 14–34, 36–39, 425, and 50–74. Reprinted by permis-
sion of the publishers.

ment. He had been, he said, on his way to his home in Santo Domingo in the New World, when something occurred which he wished to report to the Inquisition. He was duly sworn and the notary recorded his testimony as follows:

He stated that on his way from Burgos to a place called Móstoles in the jurisdiction of [the Inquisition of] Toledo he stopped at a place called Cerezo, two leagues from Somosierra on the Burgos road, and took lodgings at an inn owned by a widow named la Caballera or la Hidalga—he does not recall which. This was fourteen days ago on a Thursday night.

There he met a man whose name he does not remember. This man was of above medium height, with a rather fair, fleshy face. He wore a black sack-coat, carried a dagger, and wore a red travelling cap of the kind which pulls down over the face and neck.

This man said he was a native of Córdoba. His servant told the present witness' servant that the man had been an apothecary, that he had grown rich, had quit his work and had gone to live with the *Clavero* of Calatrava, Fernando de Córdoba; that he had taken leave of the *Clavero* and was returning to Córdoba.

The man is about forty years old and has a black beard. He had a servant with him—a well-disposed beardless youth of eighteen, who was leading a coal black colt by the reins. The colt was lame.

The man asked the present witness if he knew the licentiate Monzón in Madrid. This witness said he knew him, but that the licentiate had gone to Málaga as the magistrate's assistant and probably could not be found in Madrid. The man said he had sent the licentiate a chest with some silk and cloth clothes which the *Clavero* of Calatrava had given him to be sold [in Madrid] because they were worth little in Burgos.

Before dining, the man and this present witness sat down by the fire to chat. In the course of their conversation they began talking about Friar Martin Luther. This witness condemned Martin Luther as a heretic. The man replied that not everything which Martin Luther said was bad: Luther spoke well, for example, when he claimed there ought not to be any images; there

was no need for images; one should adore only God and the Holy
Sacrament [of the mass]. Images, the man went on, were for
simple people and not for the judicious. And in the matter of
confession Luther spoke well also, for men should confess to
God alone and not to the priests.

This witness replied: "Don't you know that priests serve in
place of God and that men are rewarded when they tell their
sins to the priest, who gives them a penance [to perform] and
then absolves them? This is the teaching of our faith. What you
say sounds like Luther, who upholds no more than that himself."

The man told this witness to stop that sort of talk, and he
went on: "Since you are criticizing me for what I say, tell me
what it means to be a Christian." To which this witness replied:
"I'm not an educated man but I am an Old Christian from far
back. A Christian believes in God—Father, Son and Holy Ghost;
three Persons and one true God. A Christian also accepts and
believes what the Holy Mother Church believes and accepts,
and don't try to make me believe anything else. On the contrary,
how about the images of Our Lady of Guadalupe and Montserrat? They are made of wood, but they have performed miracles and have freed captives from overseas. One story I have
heard in particular is about a Christian who was being held
captive overseas. He kept praying to Our Lady of Guadalupe
to free him. His Moorish master heard him and said: 'Don't think,
dog, that your Lady of Guadalupe is going to free you.' That
night the Moor placed the Christian in a large chest and made
his own bed on top of the chest. When they awoke, the Christian, the Moor, and the chest were all in Guadalupe."

The man replied that he did not believe a word of it, and that
no one would go to Hell for not believing it. This witness angrily
replied: "Look here, do you know that Our Lady descended in
body and spirit to the holy church of Toledo and gave Saint
Ildefonso a chasuble with which to say mass? Then a later archbishop wanted to put on the chasuble to say mass with. The
cathedral chapter tried in vain to persuade him not to do it. And
when he put it on he blew up with it."

The man thought this was a joke. There was no such miracles,
he said. After Our Lady went up to Heaven, She had not come
back down, nor did the Church so hold; and She had not given

any chasuble to Saint Ildefonso either. This witness then got up angrily and, refusing to talk with the man any longer, he went to check on his mule.

This witness further recalled that during the course of the discussion, the man twice claimed that there was no need for images and that he had asked this witness: "What difference is there between the images we have today and the idols of the pagans?" This witness had replied: "The pagans worshipped their images as gods, while we worship our images because they represent those who are living in Heaven." Such a question impressed this witness as very wrong.

Those present during all this [conversation] were the landlady, her son (about thirty years old), a daughter or maidservant aged twelve or thirteen, the man's servant, and the servant of this present witness—a boy named Juan, who is a native of Vizcaya. It is possible that some of these persons did not hear the whole conversation, because they kept going in and out of the kitchen.

The statement of this witness was then read back to him and he said that it was correct to the best of his recollection. Asked if he had any personal hatred for the accused, he said that he had never met him before, nor did he bear any hatred toward him. It was only that what the man had said impressed him as very wrong.

The witness was ordered to maintain secrecy about this matter.

Toledo: February 13, 1528

Two days later, the following order was issued by the Toledo Inquisition:

We, the Inquisitors against heretical depravity and apostasy in the noble city of Toledo and its archbishopric, etcetera, order you, Juan de Valenzuela, citizen of Toledo, to go to the city of Madrid or to any other place necessary, and to bring back with you [blank space left in manuscript here, to be filled in with the name of the accused], citizen of the city of Córdoba, who has been a servant of Fernando de Córdoba, *Clavero* of the Order of Calatrava. We wish to be informed by this man about certain things important to the service of God and the welfare of our

Holy Office. And if, when directed by you, this person refuses to come with you, or attempts to impose any delay upon you, we order that you bring him as a prisoner to the jail of the said Holy Office. And if, for this task, you should need aid and assistance, we further order, under pain of major excommunication and fine of 20,000 *maravedis*, that any justices or other persons, upon your request, shall give you such assistance and that they place no impediment in the way of the execution of your task.

Cerezo: February 21, 1528

. . . Alonso Diaz, the landlady's son, was much more helpful. Although he had not been present when the conversation began, he did arrive soon after, and he remembered many of the details:

When this witness arrived, they were talking about religious things and the man dressed in homespun [Rodrigo Durán] was saying: "Then you approve of Luther?" The accused replied that Luther says some very good things. When Durán, insisting that Luther was a heretic, asked the accused if images were necessary in the churches, the latter replied that they were needed for the simple, but not for judicious persons.

Durán then told the story of Saint Ildefonso and the chasuble given him by Our Lady, to which the accused replied that it was no sin to doubt such a tale. The remainder of Alonso Díaz' testimony followed closely the account given in the accusation made by Rodrigo Durán, except that the witness could not recall hearing anything said about the proper mode of confession, although he was certain that the accused might well have said that Luther spoke well on the matter of confession.

Córdoba: February 27, 1528

Unable to locate or even identify the man they sought, the Toledo Inquisitors sent a copy of the accusation to the Holy Office at Córdoba with instructions to pick up the man accused by Rodrigo Durán. On Thursday morning, February 27, Diego de Uceda was apprehended at the home of relatives and brought to the Inquisition chambers. Rodrigo Durán and his servant, Juan de Avellaneda, who had come to Córdoba to make the identification, remained in a separate room unseen by Diego de Uceda and duly swore that he was the man in question. Durán and his servant then formally repeated the accusation they had made in Toledo against Diego de Uceda and, having done their duty, resumed their journey to the New World.

The questioning of Diego de Uceda then began:

He was asked if he has seen, known, or heard of any person who has done or said anything which might be offensive to God and His Holy Catholic Faith, holding or affirming any opinion contrary to what the Apostolic Church holds, teaches, and confesses. He replied that he has no knowledge of any such thing, nor of any person who might have expressed such thoughts to him; if he had heard such things from some person who did not know any better, he would have corrected him as to the teachings of the Holy Mother Church, as God gave him to understand those teachings.

He was asked if he is guilty of having done, said or affirmed any of the above-mentioned things, and if so, that he so state and declare. He replied that he is a sinner at every moment, but in the matter of expressing or affirming opinions contrary to those held by the Holy Mother Church he does not take such things upon himself, but follows the Church.

He was asked if he knows or can think of any reason why he has been called before this Holy Office. He replied that he neither knows nor can understand; the thought did pass through his mind, however, that perhaps someone, in speaking with him, had misunderstood something he had said and had reported his words to the contrary of what they were. But he cannot recall having said anything that might be so reported. If he has said anything wrong, he submits himself to the correction of the Holy Mother Church, because he has always done so. He feels he should say this because he has seen many instances of persons being accused before the Inquisition of Toledo on the basis of subtleties in the matter of words.

He was told that if he is guilty of having said some things offensive to our Holy Catholic faith, so to declare. He replied that he has not done so, nor may it please God will he ever do so.

He was then advised by their reverences that he has been

called before this Holy Office because he has been accused of
having said, held, and affirmed a certain heretical proposition or
propositions held and affirmed by the heretic Martin Luther.
Therefore, for the love of Our Lord, he should manifest the
truth of his guilt.

He said that the only thing he has said about Luther is that
he is favorably impressed by the latter's statements to the effect
that Church officials should be poor. He does not recall having
approved any of Luther's other ideas. If he has erred in this, he
submits himself to the correction of the Holy Mother Church.
Also, he well knows that many wicked things are maintained by
Luther, and if he has spoken at all on such matters, it has been
during discussions about Luther. However, he does not remember with what persons or in what places he has had such discussions.

Diego de Uceda was then locked up in a cell so that "he
might have more time to think and to declare his guilt." When
brought out for another hearing that afternoon, he first insisted
he could remember no more than he had stated in the morning.
But under pressure from his questioners, Diego recalled something more:

He was told by their reverences for love of Our Lord to
examine his conscience carefully and declare truthfully whether
he has approved, confirmed or held the opinions and errors of
Luther, particularly if he has maintained that oral confession
need not be made to the priest but to God alone, or that there
is no need for images, or any other opinions of Luther.

He replied that all he has said about confession is that it consists primarily in a man's recognizing in his soul that he is a sinner
and feeling repentance for his sin. Then, in compliance with
the command of the Holy Mother Church, he must make confession to the priest. The principal requirement is, however, that
he first truly repent in his soul and be determined to amend his
errors and to commit no more. This is all he has said on the
matter of confession.

He did discuss the subject of confession one evening with a
priest in the presence of a canon from León, and he believes that
some other persons, overhearing parts of the discussion, mis-

understood some of his words and reported them incorrectly to the Inquisition . . . As for images, he has always maintained that they are for the sole purpose of representing the saints to the spirit of Christians. In this matter, as in that of confession, he must have been overheard and misunderstood, because what he has said about images and confession is developed in the works of Erasmus, which have been approved by Spain's Inquisitor General. As for Luther, he knows nothing about him and does not wish to, either.

He was told to reflect carefully on what he is saying—whether he has maintained that oral confession is not necessary, and that confession to God is sufficient. If so, he should so state, because he has been accused in this Holy Office of having taken such a position.

He replied that whenever the occasion has offered, he has stated his position on this matter. Especially did he do so on the evening he mentioned. It was two weeks ago at an inn [at Guadarrama] between Arjona and Baena. He was talking with the archpriest of Arjona and the canon of León was present. Those who were listening to the discussion must have caught some words which they did not properly understand, for what he said on that occasion was the same as he has just stated, and in this, as in all else, he submits himself to the correction of the Catholic Church.

He was directed to declare whether he has said that he does not believe that the images of Our Lady the Virgin Saint Mary have performed miracles. In regard to miracles, he stated that about twelve or thirteen days ago he stopped at Baena . . . at an inn near the chapel of [Our Lady of] Guadalupe. He was sitting near the landlady when an old woman approached and whispered in the landlady's ear certain things about miracles at the nearby chapel of Our Lady of Guadalupe. Unable to hear, this witness asked what the old lady was saying. The landlady told him: "She says, sir, that they put a paralyzed boy in the chapel of Our Lady and his legs straightened out." This witness then replied: "Sisters, do not waste your time on such things. As for your story about Don Juan, son of the Count, driving out the clerics because they were speaking of miracles taking place there, [I think] he did the proper thing, because miracles are performed only where there is a lack of faith, for the purpose of providing a good example. You, who are good Christians, need respect nothing except the true Sacrament of the altar. If you like relics so well, there is no better relic than the chalice where the Blood of Jesus Christ our Redeemer is consecrated, and the patina where His Holy Body is placed. . . Believe me, if you would say your beads over the chalice as you do over other relics, you would be free of any evil which might befall you."

"Do you mean," they asked, "that there is no truth to the miracles performed by Our Lady?" "I do not deny their validity," he answered, "nor do I say that Our Lady does not have the power to perform such miracles, nor that your story is not true. But even if it is true that this boy was cured—which has not been proven—you should not make so much of it until you are certain. . . ."

The accused was then asked if he has spoken with any other persons about confession or about the opinions of Martin Luther. Did he say to such other persons that oral confession is not necessary, but that one need only lament in his soul for having committed sin? Did such person or persons reprove him for speaking improperly and untruthfully? Did they tell him that sinners earn merits by confessing their sins to the priest, who are here to represent God? Did he reply to such reproof by persisting in his opinion and favoring Martin Luther? Did he tell such persons to "stop that sort of talk?"

The accused replied that when the occasion has offered he has spoken with other persons on the matter of confession. He has said that it consists principally in lamenting inwardly the errors by which we offend God, followed by oral confession to the priest in accordance with the teaching of the Holy Mother Church. In this, as in all else, he submits himself to the correction of the Holy Mother Church.

He added that whenever he has spoken on this subject, sometimes his listeners would misinterpret what he said and would tell him he was talking like Luther. He would reply: "Friend, or friends, do not deceive yourselves; the most important thing about confession is that it must be made spiritually to God," adding that after grieving in one's heart for having offended

God, then one must make oral confession at the feet of the priest. "And if you think I am wrong," he would say, "check it for yourself. That is how it was taught to me, so do not be shocked and think that I am denying oral confession."

He was asked when or where he had been reproved for saying such things, and by what persons. He said that he does not recall.

The accused was then advised that since he has been accused of denying the need of oral confession to the priest, and of the other things mentioned above, he would be given time until tomorrow to consider telling the truth so that there would be better opportunity to use mercy on him. He was then returned to his cell.

Córdoba: February 28, 1528

The following morning, Diego de Uceda was brought out of his cell for questioning a third time. He persisted in protesting his inability to recall any more than he had stated on the previous day, and that everything he had ever said on matters of theology had been in accordance with his own conscience.

He went on to point out that he was an Old Christian on both sides of the family, and there was not a drop of Jewish *converso* blood in him. The Inquisitors could ascertain all this from some old friends of his family, who would not only attest to the purity of his blood, but who would explain that Diego was not the kind of man to say frivolous things about religion. Anyone who claimed that he was, simply did not understand Diego's words or intent.

The Inquisitors of Córdoba then called four character witnesses named by Diego. They were all natives of Córdoba and old friends of the family, who had known Diego from birth. They all agreed that Diego was an Old Christian, that he had always lived a virtuous life and never gave the slightest indication of heretical tendencies. One of the witnesses noted that Diego was inclined to read a good deal. He recalled having seen Diego read some of the works of Erasmus, and he thought that this might account for Diego's present difficulties. He was positive, however, that Diego was a very good Christian. Another witness was so impressed with Diego's virtues that he was certain Diego was more inclined to the religious life than to that of a married man or courtier. On the major point, that of Diego's orthodoxy and good intentions, the witnesses agreed unanimously.

Córdoba: March 2, 1528

At noon, on March 2, a messenger left Córdoba with the following letter addressed to the Inquisition tribunal at Toledo:

We received the letter of your graces and with it the accusation against Diego de Uceda. We took action as you instructed, as you can see from the examination made of the said Diego de Uceda.

He is being held prisoner here, but we have not ordered that his property be seized because his own testimony and the information we have received about the high quality of his person have made us hesitate to take such a step.

This case is essentially a problem in the interpretation of words. In his testimony the accused says that it is customary with him in discussions to say that true confession is the inner lament to God which the sinner makes in his soul. He does not, however, deny the validity of oral confession. It is possible that the witness who made the accusation against him did not clearly understand the intent of the said Diego de Uceda when he accused him of denying oral confession.

For this reason, and also because we have received favorable accounts of his life and habits, and because he is an Old Christian of honorable family, we have suspended proceedings against him here. Having examined the witnesses and ratified their testimony, we are sending this messenger to you to advise your graces of our decision and to determine your wishes in regard to this matter.

Córdoba: March 14-23, 1528

Pending receipt of some word from Toledo, Diego de Uceda was held in jail at Córdoba. As the days dragged by and nothing happened, Diego became impatient for his release. On March 14 and March 23 he addressed petitions to the Córdoba Inquisitors, assuring them of his orthodoxy and asking that he be released.

In the first petition he referred again to his conversation at

Guadarrama with the archpriest of Arjona, insisting that he must have been overheard and his words misinterpreted. Whoever accused him obviously did not know him at all, because he was a staunch supporter of the Faith. He offered to show proof of his orthodoxy in the form of some personal possessions: a list of his sins which he had prepared to take with him to confession; excerpts he had copied from a book of miracles; a historical treatise on Mary Magdalen, which also contained miracles; an image of Our Lady which he kept for contemplation. It was obvious, he concluded, that whoever accused him of heresy was a person of poor judgment.

Diego's second petition, written nine days later, shows that his frustration and anger had increased considerably. His unknown accuser, he said, was a low and vile person, who spoke evil, stupid, and vicious words. If he had spoken wrongly, surely the archpriest of Arjona would have corrected him. Then his tone changes from haughty anger almost to abject pleading, as Diego begs them not to forget him, but to be merciful and charitable. If only they will let him go, he will promise not to leave the city—not even to leave his lodgings if they so wish.

Nine days later, Diego de Uceda was transferred to the Inquisition jail in Toledo.

The Toledo Inquisitors obviously did not shake the opinion of their colleagues in Córdoba that Diego's case warranted no further investigation. On Wednesday, April 1, the accused was transferred to the Inquisition cells of the Toledo tribunal. On the following day he was brought to the audience chamber for questioning:

He was reminded how he had been admonished by the Córdoba Inquisitors to confess the truth about certain matters given in testimony. He was once more directed to state truthfully the guilt he felt for having done or said something against our Holy Catholic Faith. In this way he could clear his conscience and assure himself of mercy.

Diego assured his questioners that his only wish was to live and die in the Catholic faith. He had already told the truth, he said, to the Inquisitors in Córdoba, about his conversation with the archpriest of Arjona and the canon of León. He was certain

that someone listening at the time had misunderstood his words.
If what he had said was wrong, he now submitted himself to
the correction of the Holy Mother Church. Perhaps he had been
out of his head at the time, or drunk, in which case he begged
for mercy and asked that he be given proper penance. He never
would consciously say anything wrong, and he could produce
witnesses who would testify to that effect.

Toledo: April 3, 1528

Diego still believed that his troubles stemmed from his conversation at Guadarrama with the archpriest of Arjona and the
canon of León. When he was returned to his cell after his first
audience, Diego prepared a lengthy letter of defense which he
submitted to the Inquisitors on the following day. Sometime in
January, while on his way from Burgos to Córdoba, he had
stopped at the inn of Guadarrama. There he met the archpriest
of Arjona and the canon of León, and the three had sat down
to chat. Other persons present were the landlady and the landlord, although he was not sure whether the latter remained
nearby all the time:

I asked the archpriest if he knew anything about Erasmus. He
said he did not, so I told him about the *Colloquies* and the *Enchiridion*, and about another work called *Imensa Misericordia
Dei*, and advised him to try to get copies. He said he had heard
that these books had been condemned, so I enlightened him on
the matter.

At that moment two or three muleteers came in and sat down
at a nearby table. I continued talking to the archpriest, urging
him to get Erasmus' writings. . . . I told him about some of the
clever things in the *Colloquies*, especially about the colloquy of
Erasmus [*sic*] and Gaspar which discusses the proper attitude
to take toward holy things. I told him what Erasmius says in
the same colloquy about confession—how the most important
thing is for the sinner to repent in his soul for having offended
God, and how the boy [Gaspar] said that he searched his thoughts
every night and if he found that during the day he had offended
Our Lord, he begged God's pardon, weeping and rending his

heartstrings, and promising to mend his ways in the future. And after this, one must make oral confession to the priest. . . .

Then I turned to the persons sitting at the nearby table and, looking at the one directly opposite me, . . . I said, "Friends, if you wish to go to Heaven, listen to me. The most important thing in confession is for the sinner to repent inwardly for his sins and to promise to mend his ways in the future. After that he should confess to the priest."

I do not recall whether I also said, as I sometimes do, that inner contrition is of such major importance that if one suddenly found himself at the point of death and was unable to find a priest to confess him, in such a case inner confession is sufficient for salvation, and that without contrition, confession to the priest itself would not suffice.

To all this the man opposite me and the other persons with him never said a word. It seems to me that ignorance combined with an unwillingness to learn is the basis of many evils, and it was the ignorance of these low-spirited men of poor judgment that made them misunderstand my words. Did they not misunderstand my conversation with the archpriest, and say that he reproved my words but that I still held to my opinion?

I also said that Erasmus was an enemy of far-fetched extravagances in religion and that the masses were too quick to accept fantasies about the appearance of Our Lady in various places. The only miracles to be believed, I said, were those officially approved by the Church, and these miracles were performed to instill faith in those who did not have it. Erasmus himself, I pointed out, says in the *Enchiridion* that persons with weak faith reverence miracles. As for images, I said that they serve no other purpose than to represent the real meaning of our faith.

Still under the delusion that he had been accused by the muleteers who had overheard his conversation with the archpriest of Arjona, Diego assailed them for being poor Christians. If they had been men of virtue and good faith, they would not have rushed to denounce him. Instead, in a truly fraternal Christian spirit, they would have asked him to elaborate and thereby availed themselves of the opportunity to be enlightened. But no, they demonstrated their wickedness and unpardonable ignorance by denouncing him for something they did not understand. They should be made to specify in detail exactly what he said that was heretical; only in this way could the truth be brought out. Diego's honor might then be restored and his wretched accusers punished for their ignorance. It was a different matter, however, if he had been denounced by the archpriest of Arjona:

In that case I admit my guilt and throw myself on the mercy of your graces, begging you to impose upon me the penance necessary for the well-being of my soul. For I consider the archpriest to be a well-informed man of prudence and good judgment and if my words seemed wrong to him, then I know that although my intentions were good, my tongue inadvertently failed to express my ideas properly, and I deserve whatever penance may be given me.

Furthermore, if there are a large number of reliable witnesses who say that I spoke foolishly and improperly, I admit my guilt and throw myself upon your mercy, begging you to give me proper penance, because I swear in the name of Our Lord and the Blessed Virgin that I do not remember ever having said the things of which I am accused. If necessary, you can check with persons who have known me all my life, and they will tell you whether I am in the habit of saying such things. . . .

Sirs, I confessed during Holy Week of last year in Valladolid in the [monastery of] the Trinity, to the licentiate Arévalo, a friar of that order. He will testify to this if you will describe my appearance to him, for I was dressed all in black. He confessed me in a chapel of the cloister after dinner, and on another day I brought him some *reales* so that he would do a certain thing for me. On the basis of this information he will testify to having confessed me.

In Burgos I confessed on All Saints Day and took communion in the monastery of Saint Ildefonso with a cleric who was priest for the nuns, and whose name is Ordóñez. On the day of the Nativity of Our Lord immediately following, he confessed me and gave me communion. You can verify this by giving him the same description as you give to the other [Arévalo], and also by reminding him that I gave him three *reales* as pittance for three masses which he was to say for me, it being my custom to go to confession, not only yearly as the Church requires, but on certain holy days during the year.

Diego then named a number of persons who, he was certain, would testify to his orthodoxy: a chaplain and an innkeeper, with whom he had discussed Erasmus when he stopped in Madrid on his journey from Burgos to Córdoba; the present chaplain of his employer Fernando de Córdoba, with whom Diego used to discuss Erasmus; his employer's former chaplain, now in a monastery at Calatrava, with whom he had also discussed Erasmus; all the members of the household of Fernando de Córdoba, as well as the *Clavero* himself, all of whom would testify that Diego was a faithful son of the Church. Furthermore, Diego added:

I state and manifest that my intention has never been other than to live and die in the Catholic faith. If I have ever done anything to the contrary it has been through my own inadvertence, and in everything I submit myself to the correction of the Holy Mother Church.

Toledo: April 4, 1528

The following day, Diego was brought to the audience chamber for the formal reading of the charges against him. He was first given one last opportunity to confess his guilt, but he stated only that he had already told the truth and had no idea how he could add to that. The prosecutor then presented the charges against him, accusing him of heresy on six counts:

First: Diego de Uceda had spoken about the teachings of the wicked heretic Friar Martin Luther, favoring and approving of those teachings like a person who believes and agrees with them. He had said and affirmed that Friar Martin Luther spoke well when he said men should confess to God alone and not to the priests. He had been reproved by a certain person who had told him that the priests are here to represent God, that men earned merits by confessing their sins to the priest, that they were thus given penance and absolved, that this was the teaching of our

Catholic faith, and that Diego de Uceda was talking like Luther. Diego de Uceda replied to this person by telling him to stop talking that way, and he persisted in his Lutheran errors.

Second: A certain person said that Luther was a terrible heretic. Diego de Uceda, defending and approving of Luther, like the heretic that he is, said that Luther's teachings were not all bad, as for example when Luther said there was no need for images and that men need worship only God and the Holy Sacrament; that images were for the simple and not for the judicious. Diego de Uceda asked this person what difference there is between the images we have today and the idols which the pagans had. When this person replied that the pagans worship their images as gods, but that Christians worship them as representing the saints in Heaven, Diego de Uceda, persisting in his error and comparing the images of the glorious saints with pagan idols, then said that images were a joke and that he did not believe in them, thereby rejecting images, as Luther does.

Third: A certain person said to Diego de Uceda that although the images of Our Lady of Guadalupe and Montserrat were made of wood, they had performed miracles and had freed captives from overseas. This person told of a Christian captive overseas who prayed to Our Lady of Guadalupe to free him. His Moorish captor heard him and said: "Don't think, dog, that your Lady of Guadalupe is going to free you." The Moor put the Christian in a chest that night to sleep, and made his own bed on top of the chest. Yet the next morning the Christian, the Moor, and the chest were in Guadalupe. Diego de Uceda replied to this that he did not believe a word of it and that images are a joke. . . .

Fourth: A certain person said that Our Lady the Holy Virgin Mary had come down in the flesh and spirit to the holy church of Toledo and had given to Saint Ildefonso a chasuble with which to say mass. A later Archbishop of Toledo had wanted to put on the chasuble to say mass in it. The cathedral chapter tried in vain to prevent him from doing so, and when he put it on he blew up with it. Diego de Uceda rejected not only the images and the miracles which God performs through the images, but even the miracles performed by Our Lady, which are well known in Spain, and particularly the miracle of Her descent into this holy church of Toledo. He said that it was all a joke, that there were no such miracles and that Our Lady, after She had ascended to Heaven, had never returned to earth, nor did the Church so hold, nor had She given the chasuble to Saint Ilde-fonso.

Fifth: Diego de Uceda has consorted and communed with heretics. He has favored and defended them. He knows many heresies and errors of heretics, about which he remains silent and covers up so that these heretics may go unpunished. He has been under sentence of major excommunication for some time, and he has perjured himself before this court.

Sixth: In addition to the above-stated charges, Diego de Uceda has done, said, held, believed, and affirmed many other heresies and errors against the Faith and he knows of other persons who have done the same.

Reserving the right to add more charges later, the prosecutor then asked that Diego be found guilty of "being an apostate heretic against our Holy Catholic Faith" and a follower of Mar-tin Luther. All Diego's property should be confiscated and turned over to the royal treasury. Diego himself should be turned over to the secular arm for execution. His descendants for two generations on the male side and for one generation on the female side should be deprived of all public and ecclesiastical offices and honors, and be declared forever ineligible to hold any such posts.

The prosecutor concluded with a demand that the accused be compelled to reply immediately to each of the charges in turn. Diego, still unaware of the source of the accusation against him, probably did as well as could be expected:

First: The accused maintains that he has already stated his position on confession, as explained in Erasmus' colloquy [*Pietas Puerilis*] between Gaspar and Erasmius. Furthermore, on this matter he has also submitted to the correction of the Church. Although he is not absolutely certain, he believes that the arch-priest of Arjona, on the night in question, asked him if Luther was still living and the accused replied that he was. In any case, he defers to the testimony of the archpriest on this point. The accused admitted that he sometimes speaks about Luther's teachings in this manner: that Luther will first say something which any good Christian can believe, and then will repeat a number of heresies in the hope that people will believe those too. The accused also believes that the other persons in the inn at Guadarrama heard the name of Luther and then the discussion about Erasmus, and assumed that everything referred to Luther. The accused maintains that he is a Catholic Christian, that investigation will prove it, and that the remainder of this charge is untrue.

Second: With regard to images, he believes that on the night in question, at Guadarrama, he might have spoken as follows: that among the wicked teachings of Luther is his denial of images; however, this is not Luther's most serious heresy, because images actually serve only as symbols of spiritual reality. The rest of this charge he denies.

In his reply to the third and fourth charges, which were based on Diego's supposed rejection of the two miracles recounted to him by Rodrigo Durán, we have the first mention by Diego himself of his conversation at Cerezo. It is little more than a passing reference, Diego having already convinced himself that his difficulties originated with the muleteers who had overheard his conversation with the archpriest of Arjona:

Third and fourth: The accused claims that he had not consciously formed any opinion on the story of the chasuble of Saint Ildefonso. One evening he was talking with some man who told him the story of the chasuble which Our Lady had given to Saint Ildefonso. Because he was expected to make some reply, the accused said that the story is well known, especially in the Archbishopric of Toledo, and there is nothing wrong with believing it, although it is generally agreed that Our Lady never came back to earth once She had ascended to Heaven. It is true, however, that God does perform miracles and there is no question about the sanctity of Saint Ildefonso because he has been canonized by the Church. If, through his own inadvertence, he said the wrong thing, he submits himself to the correction of the Holy Mother Church and begs for penance. However, he does not feel that he detracted in any way from the authority of the Holy Virgin in what he said, because he made no objection to anyone's believing the story even though it is not an article of the Catholic faith. . . .

The accused recalled that the same man had asked him if Luther did not speak in the same way. He replied that it was all right to believe the story about the chasuble, but that if it were salvation one was seeking, he should concern himself with more important matters. . . . All he remembers about the man with whom he had this conversation is that he wore gray homespun, had one eye, was on his way to the New World, and that they had this conversation at a place called Cerezo. . . .

Fifth: The accused denied that he had ever had any dealings with heretics. He was raised in the household of Fernando de Córdoba, *Clavero* of Calatrava. He has never travelled in foreign lands, but has always remained in his employer's household. The *Clavero* and all the members of his staff will testify that it is not his practice to discuss Luther.

Sixth: He completely denies this charge.

Upon completion of Diego's statement, the court ruled that he was a negativist, and returned him to his cell.

*   *   *

Toledo: May 2, 1528

On April 27, legal counsel was assigned by the Inquisition to Diego de Uceda. Five days later, in Diego's name, his counsel submitted a defense of the accused based partly on legalistic grounds:

The accusation against me is neither precise nor correct; it is general and obscure. . . .

On the basis of this same accusation I was called before the Inquisitors of Córdoba. As a faithful Catholic I answered the charges in full and was then given my freedom. Therefore I cannot properly be called to answer to the same charges again.

It cannot be proven that I have favored, approved, or held any of the evil and harmful opinions of Friar Martin Luther; on the contrary, I abhor and detest them. Much less did I ever affirm his false opinion that men need confess only to God and not to the priests. . . . For I am a Catholic Christian who firmly believes that confession to the priest is necessary for the salvation of all Christians. . . . If I did speak any words on confession at any time or place, or with any person whatsoever, I did so in a healthy Catholic spirit.

What I said was that the most important thing in confession was for the sinner to lament inwardly his sins, to repent, and to ask God's pardon. . . . This should then be followed by oral confession to the priest, and the carrying out of the penance imposed. However, because I might have said that the sinner should repent his sins and beg God's pardon . . . it does not follow that I was denying oral confession and, indeed, I never did deny it. . . .

I confess to the priest and take the Holy Sacrament two times more per year than is required by the Church. Anyone who does this certainly cannot reasonably be believed to have denied oral confession or to have fallen into Lutheran errors, as I am accused of having done. . . .

I do not recall any person telling me that Martin Luther was a terrible heretic, but even if someone had said it, I certainly would not have contradicted him and defended Luther's works. Nor would I have replied that not everything Luther said was bad, because I consider all his teachings reprehensible. If I said anything at all, it was . . . that Luther sometimes says something that seems good, in order to deceive people into believing good of his many bad and harmful teachings. . . .

I may also have said that Luther denied the validity of images, but I never said that I agreed with him. If I said anything, it was that images are for the purpose of representing to faithful Christians the saints in Heaven. This certainly is not contrary to the teachings of our Holy Catholic Faith, and if the person who heard such words had any judgment or understanding, he would agree. . . . Nor did I ever compare images with pagan idols. . . . I have always revered and venerated images in the churches, monasteries and sanctuaries. . . .

I deny the accusation that I said I did not believe Our Lady had freed captives from overseas. . . . [Contradicts some earlier testimony.] If I said anything on the subject, it was to the effect that miracles occur where it is necessary to bolster weak faith, and that faithful Christians owe their greatest veneration to the Holy Sacrament of the altar, and that there is no more truly priceless relic than the chalice where the Blood of Our Lord Jesus Christ is consecrated and the patina where His Holy Body is placed by the priest. I said that miracles should not be sworn to before they have been verified. . . .

I never said, either in public or private, that Our Lady had not given the chasuble to Saint Ildefonso. . . . What I said was that it is all right to believe such a story, and that I believed and held to the beliefs and teachings of the Holy Mother Church.

I have never said anything for which I can be accused as an apostate heretic of our Holy Catholic Faith. I have never committed nor thought of committing the crime of heresy in word or deed. . . . I am and always have been a faithful Catholic in word and deed. I have never communed with heretics, nor favored nor defended them. If I had ever known of any heresy being committed, I would not have kept silent nor covered it up. I would have exposed it so that it might be punished. . . . Therefore, I beg your graces to disregard the accusation against me as worthless, and to set me free.

Toledo: May 9, 1528

The Inquisitors of Toledo ignored Diego's supplication. On May 7 the charges against him were repeated in substantially the same form as they had been made by the prosecutor. Diego again replied to each charge. He was told that his "confession" was too general and that he would have to be more explicit if he were to expect any mercy.

Two days later, Diego requested an audience, that he might make another statement. It is obvious that Diego by this time was trying desperately to extricate himself from his difficulties:

Diego de Uceda stated that he recalled clearly that the two muleteers of Guadarrama, who have denounced him, had overheard his talk with the archpriest. They heard him say that Erasmus spoke well when he said that the most important thing in confession was one's inner feelings, and they confused this with the teachings of Luther.

This explains the statement of one of his accusers to the effect that Diego de Uceda asked him what it meant to be a Christian, because the accused has asked this question of others when they have behaved badly. [Diego de Uceda quoted] Saint John: "Blessed are they who die in the Lord, for their works will follow them." The glorious Apostle Saint Paul, he said, shows us clearly that works performed without charity are worthless, that charity is one's link with perfection, and that true Christianity lies in good works together with belief. . . .

The accused also spoke in this vein with another priest in Madrid, who was in the service of the *maestrescuela* of Toledo. This conversation took place on Sunday evening, February 2, at an inn owned by one Baena. Those present were the landlord, Baena, and a gentleman from Jaén.

The accused repeated that if those who testified against him are reliable persons of good faith, that he defers to their judgment and begs for mercy, for he knows then that his tongue has erred, though not his intent. He entrusts his fate to the consciences of the reverend Inquisitors, because he is a Catholic Christian in life, in deeds, and in works. This can be determined, he said, from all the persons he has named on a list, to be questioned as to his good intentions. . . .

The accused believes God has permitted this adversity to befall him in order that his sins might be purged. He prays to God that such is the reason for his misfortune, and to God's hands he entrusts the expediting of this affair. . . .

He was told by the Inquisitors that if he has any doubts in his heart about the sacrament of oral confession, to declare the whole truth and unburden his conscience. He replied that he swears to God and the Virgin Mary that never in his life has it occurred to him to do other than believe and love everything taught by the Holy Catholic Church.

He was told by the Inquisitors to examine his conscience carefully and declare the truth, because his reply does not satisfy the evidence against him; nor can it be believed that he would not have denied oral confession unless he did have such ideas in his heart for some time. He replied that he never has held in his heart anything other than what he has already stated, and may God help him in his adversity, because his intentions have always been of the best.

Diego was told that his testimony was not satisfactory, and he was returned to his cell. . . .

The task of locating witnesses was a long and difficult one. The first effort, made May 30, 1528, at Baena, was completely unsuccessful. The two old ladies with whom Diego claimed to have discussed miracles seemed to have vanished completely. Questioning of a number of residents of the inn at Baena shed no light on the whereabouts of these women.

It was almost a month later before any further testimony was taken. On June 23, Cristóbal Juárez, the canon of León, was questioned in his native city. Of Diego's conversation with the archpriest of Arjona at Guadarrama, Juárez said that he knew nothing, because he had gone to bed early. The next morning he had accompanied Diego and the archpriest as far as Bailén, and during the journey he had heard nothing to indicate that Diego was anything but a faithful son of the Church.

Meanwhile, Diego was becoming impatient. The same day the canon of León was being questioned, Diego requested an audience with his jailers:

He begged their graces, for love of God, to finish his case as soon as possible. He has already spent four months here and is suffering greatly from his imprisonment. Their graces replied that his case is under advisement and that it will be completed as quickly as possible.

Córdoba: July 27, 1528

Questioned the second time, the archpriest of Arjona added some details to his previous testimony of April 28:

The archpriest recalls that Diego de Uceda praised the works of Erasmus . . . saying that they were good and profitable books, and that they had been approved by a congregation of learned men in Valladolid. . . .

He remembers also that Diego de Uceda quoted Erasmus as saying that the most important part of confession is to grieve for the sin committed against God, determined to confess it to one's confessor in accordance with the requirements of the Holy Mother Church. . . .

He remembers that Diego de Uceda had much to say about

Luther and his doctrines and about images, but as the accused spoke a great deal and the archpriest was praying his hours part of the time, he did not pay close attention to what the accused was saying. . . .

He did not see or hear Diego de Uceda say anything contrary to our Holy Catholic Faith. If the accused had done so, the archpriest would have reproved him and forbidden him to go on, and he would have denounced him. He did reprove him for speaking about Erasmus because it was not seemly to speak about such things among country people and farmers. Diego de Uceda had replied that the works of Erasmus were Catholic, and had been approved, and that he was not doing wrong in talking about them. At court, he said, these works were looked on with favor and he advised this witness to buy them.

Toledo: August 20, 1528

Three weeks went by, and Diego asked for another audience:

The accused said that three months have passed since he presented his list of character witnesses, and that a total of six months has elapsed since he was brought here. The accused stated that his detention is causing him heavy losses and damage, and that he has been told nothing about what is being decided in his case. He begged his grace that his case be expedited and that he be advised of the present status of affairs so that he might decide whether it would be better to continue or to conclude the case on the basis of what has been done so far. The Inquisitor replied that the accused has already been told all that it is possible to tell him, and that he cannot be told any more at present. He will be told more a little later.

Toledo: August 22, 1528

On the twenty-second day of August of this year, Inquisitors Baltasar de Castro and Juan Yáñez were in the audience chamber. Diego de Uceda, having requested an audience, appeared and told their graces that he begged them, for love of God, to dispatch his case quickly, because he has no father or mother or brother, or anyone else to help him. Their graces replied that they have already told him that they want to finish his case as soon as they possibly can, and that they make the same reply to him now as before.

Madrid: August 22, 1528

Diego de Uceda counted heavily on good character references from the household of his employer. His friends there probably meant well, but their testimony might have given Diego some uneasy moments:

[Fernando de Córdoba, *Clavero* of Calatrava] said that Diego is of good birth and is an Old Christian. He knows this because he has had Diego de Uceda as a member of his household, and because he knows his relatives in Córdoba, who are all of good birth and Christian blood. He said Diego de Uceda never spoke or acted contrary to our Holy Catholic Faith, nor did he ever praise the works of Luther. . . . This witness has noticed that Diego de Uceda was always fond of reading and talking about subtleties. . . .

[Juan García de Henares] said that Diego de Uceda has always lived a pure Christian life in the thirteen years this witness has know him. . . . This witness has always considered Diego de Uceda to be a God-fearing Catholic Christian, who attends mass and matins, and performs the works of a good Christian, such as praying and giving alms. However, this witness has often heard Diego de Uceda say some things about our Holy Faith which did not seem proper. . . . He does not recall just what they were except that Diego de Uceda, in reading the books of Erasmus in Spanish, quoted many foolish things which seemed improper to those who heard him. This witness and the other members of the household who heard these things reproved Diego for what he said. Diego replied that they did not know what they were talking about. This witness has never heard Diego de Uceda praise the works of Martin Luther. . . .

[Diego Cabeza de Vaca] said that Diego de Uceda has always lived purely like any good Christian. This witness never saw him do anything wrong; in fact, he has seen Diego de Uceda scold blasphemous persons. . . . He has never heard Diego say anything against our Holy Faith nor against the teachings of the Holy Mother Church. He has never heard him praise Martin

Luther. If Diego ever had done or said anything against the Faith or the teachings of the Church, this witness believes he would have known it, because he has had many conversations with Diego. In fact, he has heard Diego talk several times about becoming a friar in the Geronimite Order. . . .

[Francisco de Ayala] has always considered Diego de Uceda to be a good Christian because he has always performed good Christian deeds, such as giving alms, going to sermons, and reproving others for wrongdoing. This witness has never seen Diego do anything which would indicate he was a bad Christian, except that he has seen Diego read the books of Erasmus and dispute about some things which this witness did not want to hear. . . . Once, when Diego was reading the *Enchiridion*, he quarreled with the other servants and with a cleric who said mass for the *Clavero*. The argument was about confession, and Diego said that when one got up in the morning, he should confess to God in his heart, because if he died such confession would be sufficient. This witness has often heard Diego talk this way. . . .

[Alonso de Paz] has always considered Diego de Uceda to be a good God-fearing Christian of pure habits. . . . The accused regularly attends mass and sermons, visits churches and worships images. He has given good advice to this witness and this witness has never known him to do the contrary.

Toledo: August 27, 1528

Having requested an audience, Diego de Uceda was brought before Inquisitor Baltasar de Castro. In the presence of his counsel, the accused stated that he has thoroughly searched his memory since his imprisonment, and he can recall no more than what is already contained in the confession which he made before the Inquisitors at Córdoba.

Toledo: November 6, 1528

On this date, the following persons assembled in the audience chamber of the Holy Office:

Baltasar de Castro, Inquisitor
Juan Yáñez, Inquisitor
Pedro de la Peña, Vicar and Ecclesiastical Judge Ordinary

Alonso Mejía, canon of Toledo
Doctor Jiménez Paniagua
Friar Toribio de Oropesa
Friar Miguel de Arratia

After examining the trial records of Diego de Uceda,
They unanimously stated their opinion and vote to be that
Diego de Uceda be put to torture to determine whether he said
the words attributed to him, and with what intent he said them.

Toledo: November 10, 1528

The trial of Diego de Uceda had reached the point where
Diego's whole future hung in the balance, and Diego himself,
solitary in his cell, sensed the critical nature of his situation. He
had done everything possible to clear himself. His friends and
neighbors had testified in his behalf. He had tried to recall and
explain everything which might have led to his imprisonment.
His life, his fortune, and most important of all, his honor—all
these were at stake. What more could he do to convince the
Inquisitors of his piety and orthodoxy?

He would make a last great effort. On November 10, he sent
a long letter to the Inquisitors:

For love of Our Lord do not wonder at my importunity, for
I find myself gravely wounded in body and spirit by the testimony which has been offered against me. I am particularly
aggrieved by the statements of those two muleteers. I am even
more disturbed at seeing this farce continued so long because
of the consideration given to the excuses for knavishness and
wicked error of which they have accused me and maintain
against me. For this, I can justly call out to God, asking vengeance for such a wrong and insult; and also because, as the
common saying goes, although the speaker proposes evil, the
listener should be prudent and discreet. Consider that I am a
Catholic Christian, well grounded in the Faith. I know and hold
firmly and faithfully, as a Catholic, all that is contained in the
Faith. I believe firmly and truly all that the communion of the
Holy Mother Roman Apostolic Church holds, believes, preaches,
and confesses.

At baptism I promised to guard this faith, and as a faithful believer, to die in it and for it. I know that the principal substance of the Faith consists of the Incarnation of the Son of God. This article is the beginning and foundation of the Holy Catholic Faith. Thus it was always divinely revealed and believed so that the faithful might always be saved. And this truth is so high and so lofty that it completely surpasses all human understanding and thought, as Saint John the Baptist shows us. Although he [*i.e.*, John the Baptist] was sanctified in the womb of his mother and was the son of such good parents, he said that he was not worthy to loosen the strap of the shoe of Jesus Christ. In teaching others the manner of the union of the Divine Nature with the human, he confessed that understanding was not sufficient, but that we must also believe well and faithfully.

God wishes all men to be saved; and the way of salvation and of coming to good fortune is the mystery of the Incarnation of the Son of God and the article and mystery mentioned above. He decided to reveal this truth for all time to men so that in all time they might be saved.

At the beginning of the world and of creation God revealed this truth to the first man, Adam, and brought this knowledge and faith to the good during all the first age until the sainted Noah, which was the end of the first age and the beginning of the second. After the flood, Noah taught this truth and revelation to his children and grandchildren and descendants. As Noah's lineage multiplied greatly and spread throughout the world, this knowledge and faith were gradually forgotten and each man began to make his own god like those who made gods of clay.

Then God took Abraham from his land and brought him to the Promised Land, and revealed to Abraham, expressly and clearly, this mystery of the Incarnation, and swore to him that from his seed and lineage would be born the Savior and Messiah whom God would send to save the world. Later, after a long time, this promise and revelation were revealed and renewed to King David who came from the lineage of Abraham, and God swore to David that from his seed and lineage would be born the Messiah, who was the Son of God, made man by the assumption of the flesh. God revealed to the world in general this secret of the Incarnation through the prophets, all of whom wrote principally of this lofty secret and mystery of the Incarnation of the Son of God.

In addition to this, the article most difficult to believe was that of the Holy Trinity, and thus it was shown to the world through corporal demonstration, in the baptism which Christ received at the hand of Saint John the Baptist, in the voice of the Father which was heard there, and in the Son in the flesh, and in the coming of the Holy Spirit in the form of a dove over the baptized Christ, Son of God.

This article of faith the Church likewise declares and confesses very often, every time that it gives glory to the Father, and Son, and Holy Spirit. I hold to this article and I believe in the unity of the Three Persons in one divine essence of a God who is the true Creator of all things visible and invisible.

Believing and loving all this truth, I know and truly hold that the Catholic faith and the Church are built on a foundation and pillar which is stronger than either the heavens or the earth, which pillar is that Jesus Christ Our Savior is the Son of the living God, Son of the Virgin Our Lady, and therefore is truly God and truly man. And in this and on this truth the Catholic Church and faith are founded.

Our Savior spoke thus when He asked His disciples what they were saying about Him, and the Apostle Saint Peter replied for himself and in the name of all the apostles: "Thou art Christ, the Son of the living God," and the Savior said to Saint Peter: "Neither flesh nor blood hath revealed it to thee; that is, no man revealed it, but My Father who is in Heaven revealed it, because all the faith comes through divine revelation," and He continues: "On this rock, that is, on this confession in which thou said 'Thou art Christ, Son of the living God,' I will build My Church."

And so the Church is based on the articles of the Faith and the ecclesiastical sacraments and no one can establish any other foundation except that which is already established, which is Jesus Christ. Thus all the Catholic faith is built and affirmed in this and upon this absolutely true and firm foundation, which is that Jesus Christ is the Son of the living God, and is therefore God eternal, and He is also truly man, Son of the Virgin Our Lady. To deny or disbelieve any part of this, namely, that Jesus

Christ is eternal God, Son of God the Father, and that He is man, created in the world and born of the Virgin, is equally dangerous and is destructive of the Church and the Catholic faith which are founded upon this.

Holding this as a sure and true foundation of our faith, we must believe fourteen truths, or articles, which are based upon this. Seven pertain to divinity, or to Jesus Christ as He is God; the other seven to humanity, or to Jesus Christ as He is man. And these fourteen articles are fourteen truths founded on the above-mentioned foundation; and in these truths the Church and all our Holy Catholic Faith are founded.

The first article and truth is that there is only one God—real and eternal and perfect sovereign and infinite, and not many gods. The second, that in this Divine Essence which is one and indivisible and eternal there are Three Persons—Father, Son, and Holy Spirit—and thus in one Divine Essence there is a Trinity of Persons, and the Father is God, and this is the second article. And the Son is God—this is the third article. And the Holy Spirit is God—this is the fourth article. Thus there is one single God and Three Divine Persons—Father, Son, and Holy Spirit.

Because this God is perfect sovereign and infinite and pure goodness, He created all things visible and invisible in order to communicate to them His goodness and perfection, to the extent that they were able to receive them—and this is the fifth article, namely, that God created all things visible and invisible. And because He is pure and absolute goodness, He gives grace and forgives sins—and this is the sixth article, which comprises all things relating to human sanctification. Likewise, for the reason stated above, God will make a general resurrection and He will give, forever, glory to the good and punishment to the wicked —and this is the seventh article or truth pertaining to divinity.

In regard to Christ as man, we believe seven additional truths. First, that He was conceived in the glorious womb of the Holy Virgin Mary, Our Lady, through the sole agency of the Holy Spirit. Second, that He was born true God and man, She remaining always a virgin. Third, that of His own free will, He offered Himself death and He suffered and died on the Cross to redeem us and save us by His death. Fourth, that His body was buried in a new grave and His spirit descended into Hell and brought out the holy fathers from there. Fifth, that He was resurrected in spirit and body on the third day. Sixth, that forty days after the Resurrection, He ascended in body and spirit into Heaven where He sits at the right hand of God the Father. Seventh, that on the Judgment Day He will come to judge all the world.

In these articles and truths above stated and in the ecclesiastical sacraments are founded the Holy Church and Catholic faith. It remains to name the sacraments, which are seven. The first, Baptism; the second, Confirmation; the third, Penance; the fourth, the Eucharist; the fifth, Extreme Unction; the sixth, Holy Orders; the seventh, Matrimony. In regard to the excellences and graces which are given us by our knowledge of each of these articles, I leave this to the theologians, who are the teachers of the spiritual life. For myself, being a simple man, it is sufficient to believe firmly in spirit and heart what I have here stated, holding with all that the Church holds and believes.

In regard to the third sacrament, which is Penance, since on that point my good name has been impugned, with the help of Our Lord and the grace of the Holy Spirit, I will venture to say what God gives my poor intellect to understand and feel about it, so that I might thereby praise Him who created us and then redeemed us by His suffering and death and by that blood and water which emanated from the opening in His Holy Side, which gives efficacy and potency to the above-mentioned sacraments of the Catholic Church. May it please Him to give me grace to explain what I feel about such a lofty good as we have.

Priests are instituted as arbiters between God and ourselves, and oral confession is made to them for absolution of sins. Before the law of Christ was established, it was not possible to grant absolution, because the keys had not yet been given, by virtue of which keys the priests can now absolve sinners, and through which they possess the authority attached to Christ's Passion. Nor was the gate of Heaven open before that time. And in the sacrament of confession the formal and major part is the absolution by the priest, given by virtue of the power of the keys, which represent the law of Christ.

Before the Incarnation, God, as pure spirit, was invisible, and so at that time interior confession and recognition of one's sins were sufficient. But after the Incarnation, because God made Himself a visible man, both oral and interior confession have become necessary, through which we may conform ourselves to Him in the spirit through the faith, and outwardly through oral confession. And because Christ, as man, by His Passion acquired lordship and mastery over all men, He was constituted judge of the living and the dead; and because He is not among us in bodily presence, He left His vicars, to whom He gave His keys and power to absolve and to bind, which could not have happened before His Passion.

Oral confession was also instituted as an imitation of Christ, for according to the Apostle Saint Peter, Christ suffered for us, leaving us as an example that we imitate Him and follow His footsteps; that is, that we suffer, since He suffered for us. And because when we sin we lose shame in the sight of the ever-present God and of His holy angels, it is fitting that we humble ourselves before His vicar and that we freely confess our guilt, and thus receive confusion and shame. And likewise, because by sinning we scorn the Passion which Christ received for us, we therefore humble ourselves before His vicar so that he may absolve us by authority of the keys, which contain the authority and virtue of the Passion of Christ. And likewise because Christ humbled Himself before the judge and was judged for our redemption, we humble ourselves before the priest who is His judge and vicar, so that he may judge us and absolve us of sin and condemn us to whatever penance he may wish to impose. And likewise because Christ was accused by false witnesses, we humble ourselves before the priest, so that we may be accused by our own consciences, which are divine witnesses. And likewise because Christ was stripped of all His clothing and placed on the Cross in shame and confusion, and suffered the greatest punishment in order to save us, we, in imitation of Him, place ourselves naked before His vicar, opening and declaring our consciences to His vicar, and receiving from him great confusion and shame, which is a great punishment, awaiting his judgment and sentence. And likewise because the Divine Word humbled Himself by taking on human nature, we humble ourselves before His vicar, and we humble our speech by speaking against ourselves.

In this way we are moulded and likened to and brought into conformity with Christ, who suffers for us. And consequently we are incorporated into Him and receive unto ourselves the virtue and fruit of His Passion, as members of the body of which He is the head, and thus we receive grace and infinite good.

When the sinner hears the cry of God and examines himself inwardly, knowing that he has offended God who created him and redeemed him, and it weighs upon him because he has offended God, and he proposes not to offend Him from that moment on, in so far as his strength allows, and to confess his sins and ask God's pardon; then, at that moment, God sends His grace into that soul, by which grace his sins are remitted and pardoned. This is the greatest gift we sinners on this earth have. And thus no sinner has any excuse before God, because although the sinner, after he sins, loses God's grace and cannot recover it by himself, God freely gives His grace to all creatures who wish to receive it. The sinner must do what is within his capacity, that is, grieve because he has offended God and propose not to offend Him again, and confess his sins. Thus the sinner has no excuse for his damnation. And because this gift was so great and so easy to obtain because of the infinite clemency and goodness of God, there always will remain in the soul, remorse of conscience which in Holy Scripture is called the worm, because the conscience keeps gnawing, reminding the sinner how easily he might be saved if only he wished. All this is true of the wicked and foolish and will be a most weighty burden to them *in saecula saeculorum.*

Sirs, for love of Our Lord, forgive the boldness of my long discourse. If in some parts I do not speak as well as I should, may my words be amended and corrected by your great prudence and nobility. For my intention is only to make properly understood my innocence in the face of the wicked evil which has been placed against me by the wickedness of those two muleteers.

I beg you as a favor, sirs, to render me full justice for the great offense done to me. Anyone who has spoken of the things which I have discussed in this letter knows very well how to believe and hold such things as a faithful and Catholic Christian, which I am, although I am an unworthy sinner who transgresses the commands of Our God, but with confidence in what I have said, hoping to be saved.

I also beg you as a favor, sirs, to give me my freedom, even though you may not render a decision in this matter immediately, since you tell me there have been delays caused by those two muleteers. For I, sirs, am well known and I am not guilty of the charge for which I am brought here. And I will wait around until this matter is cleared up.

Being here is a living death for me, being held here for so long, like an animal in a cage, always locked in except when your jailer brings me to the audience chamber, and leads me before you like someone leading cattle to the slaughter, or like those who observe the law of Moses. Since we are all Old Christians, for love of Our Lord, make all possible haste, as I am well known and a person of trust. I will give evidence of myself whenever I am asked to do so, of being a good Christian. In doing what I ask, you will be doing a service to God and a great favor and honor to me. If not, I will be eternally aggrieved, while your graces remain the lords.

Toledo: November 11, 1528

Had Diego's letter convinced the Inquisitors of his orthodoxy? Perhaps they were still wondering about some inconsistencies in his testimony. Perhaps they did not appreciate the mitigating circumstances under which he had been required to testify. The following day Diego addressed another letter to the Inquisitors. He was, he said, greatly distressed and tormented over the delays in his case. He had persistently told the truth from the time of his first testimony in Córdoba. If he had been guilty of the things of which he was accused, he would have admitted it and taken his punishment. But to confess a crime he did not commit would be a mortal sin, for which his punishment would be far greater.

Diego could not understand why the Inquisitors refused to believe him. Could it be that they doubted his word because the persons whom he had named as trustworthy witnesses were the very ones who had accused him? If such were the case, he begged their graces to consider the following extenuating circumstances under which he had been required to testify:

All this was due to my own weakness, resulting from the many admonitions made to me to confess, and from the fear which overcame me because of the machinations and equivocations prompted by the devil. I was especially fearful that I might be overcome by the very wickedness of which I was accused by a crowd of witnesses. It is impossible for me to remember how this misunderstanding developed, since the testimony against me was based on the misunderstanding of one person, who persuaded another person to believe that falsity was rooted in me.
. . .

When the archpriest of Arjona and I were together [in the inn at Guadarrama], two travelers came in. One was a youth and the other an older man. As far as I know the youth was a muleteer and the other man was a workman. These are the ones I have always referred to as muleteers, because they came in together. And, as I say, sirs, I feared that as there were two of them, there might be more, and what the devil sowed in their minds he might sow in the minds of others.

His present predicament, Diego said, marked the first time he had ever been involved in a lawsuit. Never having had any experience with the law, he was naturally very upset and fearful of what might happen to him. In his effort to clear himself, he had tried to explain away the accusations against him by recalling everything he might ever have said that had any bearing on his case. In such a state of fear and confusion he naturally had contradicted himself, which was probably why the Inquisitors doubted the validity of his testimony. Of one thing, however, Diego was absolutely certain:

I am a Catholic Christian, as I have always sworn and stated. If in any way or manner I said anything to indicate the contrary, either in my testimony at Córdoba or here in Toledo, which does not conform to the Holy Catholic Faith and doctrine of the holy and Catholic doctors . . . I did so through ignorance and inadvertence and not through any evil intention. And I submit both myself and whatever words I may have spoken, to the correction of the Holy Apostolic Faith, the mistress of truth, whose function it is to correct errors touching on the Faith. I also submit to correction by your graces as ministers of the Faith, because I know and hold truly that the seven sacraments of our Holy Church and Catholic faith are divine instruments through which are communicated to us the virtue and merits of the Passion of the Savior, and that these sacraments are the outward manifestations of the faith which we carry in our souls.

The sacrament of confession and all the other ecclesiastical sacraments were instituted by Christ Our God, who is both God and man and bestower of the law of grace. Therefore they are divine and not human law, and thus Christ said: "If one of you become sick, go and seek out the priests and you will be anointed with the oil of penance, by means of which you will be saved."

So I beg your graces to remember that we are all Old Christians made out of the same kind of clay. Do not think, however, that for this reason I would have failed to tell the straightforward truth. As a mortal I am in danger of death at any moment and I would not risk condemning my soul completely to Hell by lying.

Look, sirs, I have given proof of my honor as best I could, being what I am [i.e., a courtier, obliged to travel constantly with the court]. If I were something else, I might have given more abundant proof and cited the names of confessors for a longer period of time. But because I have spent my life at court, as you know, I could refer only to the few confessors I named, and even then I had to provide a description of myself so that they could identify me when they were questioned.

What they and the other witnesses said, for my heavy sins, I have not been able to find out. But I know that I have been a Christian and that I did not say what they have accused me of saying, but that the truth is just as I stated in Córdoba. I beg you, sirs, to remember how in Córdoba I called to the attention of the Inquisitors a memorandum of mine which I believe they saw. I used this memorandum [i.e., a list of his sins] so I could clear my conscience by confessing properly at Lent. I did the same thing before other confessions, in order to bolster my memory, not wanting to neglect anything which would enable me to recall everything. You must have learned about this from those confessors whose testimony has been taken, because I made it a point to let each of them know how anxious I was to confess all my sins. . . .

I beg you, sirs, to have brought before you, from some book-seller, a book called *Morning Star of the Christian Life*, printed in Castilian by order of a bishop of Coria in the time of the Catholic Monarchs. If you will read the chapter—I believe it is chapter 106—which speaks of the inner pulsation of the spirit, you will see what my intention was in my conversation with the archpriest of Arjona when I referred to the above-mentioned colloquy of Erasmus. You will also find what I was saying in other chapters, from chapter 100 and following, where the book speaks of confession. This book also contains all the sacraments of our law of grace, and this is as it should be because it might be said that I learned to read from this book. [So, even if] you do not look at the *Colloquies* [you can find my ideas in the *Morning Star of the Christian Life*].

I know what you will reply to me, sirs: "All this is true enough, but it does not meet with our entire satisfaction because the witnesses state that you said these other things." To this I reply: "Let God's mercy suffice," and I take Him as my judge. I can do no more; I have given all the satisfaction I possibly can give. No more can be done, except that I beg you, sirs, to re-member how the witnesses who accuse me say that when I was speaking with a certain person I happened to say, among other things, what they accused me of. Since they testify by hearsay, I am quite certain that there cannot actually be anyone who said that I spoke with him personally such improper words as they say I had said.

In all this, sirs, I charge your consciences to consider the great harm which has been done to me by having held me for such a long time as you know it has been. No provision was ever made to take testimony from the witnesses named by me until I, through my importunities, asked many times to have this done. Then depositions were taken from those persons with the court in Madrid. After that, at my request, a messenger was sent to Old Castile to take testimony from my confessors, in which testimony was included the story about what I said in regard to the descent of Our Lady to give the chasuble to Saint Ildefonso.

I have already admitted this, sirs, that I did say this, and it weighs on my soul and heart that I did say it, because truthfully I did not know how firmly this story was believed. In saying that it was all a joke, I was referring only to what the witness told me about an archbishop who had blown up when he put on the chasuble in spite of being told not to do so. That is what pains me, and also because I spoke erroneously and scandalously to my neighbor. For this I beg your graces for mercy.

I have all the Bulls of indulgence which have been granted by the Faith and the Roman Apostolic Church from the first Bull of the Crusade—granted in 1515—until the last one, which was granted for the building of Saint Peter's in Rome, or rather for the reconstruction of the church. In this and all the preceding Bulls many and great indulgences are granted. Among them is a plenary indulgence for the day of Our Lady on February 2, and also for the day of the Apostle Saint Matthias on February 24. Let it be considered whether I might rightfully have spiritual dispensation of any guilt [which I might have incurred] in what I said about the descent of Our Lady; because on the days to which those indulgences apply, it is my custom to visit the churches expressly for that purpose [of receiving plenary indulgence]. (I also attend church on many other days, and on all days that I possibly can.) These two indulgences came *after* I spoke the above words, all this having happened in the present year of 1528.

After reading this letter, the Inquisitors had Diego brought to the audience chamber:

Their graces instructed the accused to tell the truth about what he had done and said against our Holy Faith, and they warned him once more to tell the truth. The accused replied that he had nothing to add to what he had already stated. Their graces then said that his case had been studied and it was agreed he should be put to torture; therefore they admonished him to tell the truth.

The accused replied that in that case he would confess he had said it, although he really had not. He was told by their graces that he should hold to the truth, and that if he had said what he was accused of, to confess and clear his conscience by telling the truth. However, if he was sure he had not made such statements, he was not to testify falsely by saying that he had. The accused replied that if they were going to torture him, he would now state that he had said it, and that he had told the truth on oath before the Inquisitors of Córdoba. The Inquisitors then pronounced sentence of torture. . . .

The accused was taken down to the torture chamber. Their graces admonished him to tell the truth, declaring that if, under torture, he should die or be wounded, or shed blood, or be mutilated, it would be his own fault and responsibility. Diego de Uceda replied that he had never been in error, that if he had said it, he had done so inadvertently and through ignorance, as the witnesses had accused him, and that he could say no more.

Asked where he had said it, he replied that he had said it when talking with the archpriest of Arjona, and also in Madrid, in a conversation with the cleric who was in the service of the *maestrescuela* of Toledo, and that he might have said it in other places; if the witnesses had said that such was the case, then it was true that he had and he could do no more; and if the witnesses were Christians they were telling the truth, and he admitted that he had said it.

He was asked with what intent he had spoken about confession, what words he had used, and in what way he had used them. He replied that since the witnesses had said so, and if they were Christians, then he admitted that he had said it the way they had claimed, and that he had said it in many places, and that he had said it is not necessary to confess to the priest. He said this, sighing and moving his arms as if his words were forced out of him.

Being admonished to tell the truth, he replied that he had said it. He was then stripped down to his undershirt. He said it was true that he had said it; then he asked how he could confess to saying something he did not recall. His arms were then tied with a hemp cord and he was stretched out on a wooden trestle. While his arms were being tied, he was admonished to tell the truth. He replied that he had said what the witnesses had claimed. He was told to state in what way he had said it. He replied that as God was his witness he could not recall, but he confessed to having said it, and that he had erred in having said it; he had thought at the time that he was speaking well but he had spoken wrongly, and his bad speech now weighed more with their graces than his good thought, and he asked them to have pity on them.

His thighs and arms were then tied and the cords being twisted, he was admonished to tell the truth. He cried: "Stop it, I'll tell; I'm dying; stop it, I'll tell." And then he said that he had said it fifteen hundred times, and that Martin Luther had said that it was not necessary to confess, and that there was no need for images, and that contrition was sufficient; he had said this to the archpriest of Arjona, and in Madrid to the cleric in the service of the *maestrescuela* [of Toledo]. Also, on the road from Burgos, he had said these things to some people and particularly to two people whose names he did not know. Also, in Cerezo he had spoken with a one-eyed man who had said he was on his way to the Indies. He had told this man that Our Lady the Virgin Mary, after She had gone to Heaven, had not come back down to earth. This man said that Our Lady had brought a chasuble to Saint Ildefonso and that an archbishop who had insisted on wearing it had blown up. The accused had replied that this was a joke and that he did not believe a word of it.

He was asked how this discussion had started. He said that in the name of God he could not remember, and that it was true that he had said it and that he had believed oral confession was unnecessary and that it was necessary only to feel contrition in the soul. Asked why confession was not necessary, he said that contrition alone was enough for salvation without one's having to confess his sins to the priest. He believed he had spoken these words in Cerezo to the one-eyed man he mentioned.

He was told to state to what persons he had spoken about this and in what places, and how many times, and how long he had had this idea in his mind. He said that in Burgos a year or two ago he had spoken on this subject with [Francisco de]Ayala, [Diego] Cabeza de Vaca and [Juan García de]Henares, servants of the *Clavero* of Calatrava. He had told them that contrition without oral confession was sufficient for salvation. They had told him not to say such things, and they had reproved him for it. He had also discussed this matter many times with other persons whom he had met on the road. He could not remember how many times, although he believed it must have been seven or eight times, and he added that he had believed what he had said and discussed.

He was asked how he had fallen into this error. He said it was from hearing other persons talking about and condemning the teachings of Luther. He was [again] told to state how he had fallen into this error. He said it had come from within himself. He was asked if he had read it in some book or had heard it from some person. He said he had not read it in any book, but he had heard many people talk about it and it had made an impression on his weak judgment.

He was asked how long he had held this error. He replied that he had held this error until he had been seized and admonished in this Holy Office, and that now he believed oral confession to the priest is necessary. He was asked if, since the time he had held that it was not necessary to confess to the priest and that inner contrition for one's sins was sufficient, he had confessed to any priest. He replied that he had confessed five times since then. He was asked if on those five occasions he had told the priest about this error which he had now confessed. He said that he had confessed it to the priests. He was asked if they had absolved him from this sin and had counselled him to avoid it, and if he had promised to do so. He replied that they had so done and had advised him to avoid this sin. Asked why he had not avoided that error when his confessors had told him to, he replied that it was due to his own poor judgment.

He was asked why he had confessed his sin on these occasions when he was certain he could be saved without confessing his sins to the priest. He replied that he had been in doubt and sought to be advised by the confessors as to what was proper for him to believe.

He was asked if he knew of any person who had held the same error. He said he knew of none. He was asked for what reason he had not confessed to this error when questioned under oath by the Inquisitors, or during the time of his imprisonment. He said he had not been able to remember what to say and he had been afraid. Asked what he had been afraid of, he said that he had feared penance, punishment, and torture. They asked him if he was saying what he now said and confessed through fear of torture or because it was the truth. He replied that he was saying it because it was the truth. He was admonished to hold to the truth and not to give false testimony through fear, but to tell only the truth and to hold to it. He said that it was all true.

He was asked if during the time he had held the belief that one could be saved merely by repenting his sins without confessing them to his confessor, he had known and believed that the Church held the contrary. The accused failing to reply, his bonds were loosened. He then said that he had known it. He was asked if he had decided to hold to his belief even though the Church taught the contrary. He replied that he had not, and that he had known that the Church taught the contrary.

It was ordered that the torture be ended.

Toledo: November 13, 1528

Two days after his confession under torture, Diego de Uceda requested an audience:

He said that everything he had admitted concerning oral confession he had said because of fear of torture. . . . He never had denied the sacrament of penance. He never had spoken of nor praised the teachings of Martin Luther. . . . Whatever he had said, he had said nothing against our Holy Catholic Faith.

Their graces ordered that his confession under torture be read to him. . . . He was asked if what was read and what he had confessed and stated under torture were true. He said he swore to God and His Blessed Mother that it was not true, and that it had all been said through fear of torture. He never had denied oral confession; rather he had praised it. Everything he had said under torture was said to give the expected answers to the questions which were asked him so often by Inquisitor Juan Yáñez, and he now renounced his confession under torture. If necessary, he was prepared to die for the truth, and he never had denied the said sacrament of penance.

Diego de Uceda was returned to his cell. For the next three months his case rested.

Toledo: February 12, 1529

On this date the following persons convened in the audience chamber of the Holy Office at Toledo:

Baltasar de Castro, Inquisitor
Juan Yáñez, Inquisitor
Pedro de la Peña, Vicar and Ecclesiastical Judge Ordinary
Blas Ortiz, canon of Toledo
Friar Antonio Pizarro
Friar Alonso de Paredes
The Licentiate Falcón

They examined the case of Diego de Uceda, particularly the sentence of torture and its results, and the renunciation made later by Diego de Uceda, and the proofs against him. They unanimously stated that their vote and opinion was that Diego de Uceda should appear on the scaffold as a penitent on the day of the *auto de fe,* that his sentence should be publicly read there, and that he abjure *de vehementi* and that penance be imposed *in bonis ad arbitrium inquisitorum* and [also under the] ordinary [ecclesiastical jurisdiction].

Toledo: May 4, 1529

Pending his appearance at the *auto de fe,* Diego de Uceda was released on bail, March 6, 1529, on condition that he make his headquarters at the monastery of Saint Catherine in Toledo. In two subsequent petitions (March 19 and April 17) Diego requested permission to leave the monastery, and on April 17 he was allowed the freedom of the city.

Meanwhile, Diego had been searching his soul. Perhaps there were other things buried so deep in his conscience that he had long since forgotten them. While awaiting his summons to make public abjuration at an *auto de fe,* Diego examined his past with scrupulous care and on May 4, 1529, he sent a long letter to the Inquisitors:

I, Diego de Uceda, in this city by order of your graces, wish to state that the following has come to my recollection. In 1524, on the evening of Holy Thursday, I was residing in Burgos in a house where my employer, don Fernando de Córdoba, the present *Clavero* of the Order of Calatrava, was staying. I happened to be passing by the side door of the stable when I heard one of the slaves of the *Clavero* talking. This man was a white *morisco* named Fernando, who had been a Christian for well over twenty years. He was talking with another slave of the *Clavero*, a negro who had been baptized about seven or eight years before. The two of them being there together, I heard the white one, Fernando, say to the negro, who was also named Fernando: "Look how Christians say to put God, who be in Heaven, in the tabernacle [where the Sacrament is], and there to lock Him in with the drunks." (He spoke in this fashion because he did not know our tongue very well.)

When I heard this I went upstairs where I found Francisco de Ayala, the majordomo of the *Clavero*, and I said to him: "I just heard white Fernando talking with black Fernando," and I told him what I had heard. The majordomo summoned the white slave, berated him and made him retract what he had said. We told the black slave, who was practically a savage, of the deception and wickedness that the other had practiced on him, and by our good words we put him on the road to the true doctrine.

The white Fernando denied he had said such a thing and said he believed in the Holy Sacrament of the altar. This Fernando was a man who often used to drink wine and get drunk, although when I heard him say this he was, as I recall, sober and aware of everything. He was often sober and was a reasonable man when not under the influence of wine. This slave is not presently attached to the household of the *Clavero*, having left it some time ago in Burgos, and he has not been found. I heard him speak these words in just the way I have stated.

I was not aware that I might have been obliged to tell this to the Inquisition, or I would have reported it to the Inquisitors at Valladolid in whose jurisdiction it happened. It grieves me that I did not know my duty, for the salvation of his soul and the greater satisfaction of my own. So as not to have this on my conscience I am now speaking out in this way, because these New Christians have very bad doubts [about the Faith]. I beg Our Lord to forgive my negligence, resulting from my ignorance and lack of knowledge, which does not free me of blame before His Divine Majesty. I also beg your graces' forgiveness if in this matter I have incurred any penalty, because I want all possible security for the salvation of my soul, and to prevent the devil from being able to accuse me of this on the day of judgment.

In February of last year, while I was travelling from Burgos to Córdoba, I came to the village of Aldea del Rey, which is located in this Archbishopric of Toledo and belongs to the *Claveria* of the Order of Calatrava. Among the affairs with which I was charged, was a task which my employer, the *Clavero* of Calatrava, had directed me to perform. I was to speak about a certain matter with the priest of this village. This priest was Friar Juan Gallego, of the Order of Saint Peter.

After I had spoken with him about the matter entrusted to me, I spoke with Gaspar de Baena, the majordomo of the *Clavero* in that place. Because my instructions from the *Clavero* had to do with an agreement about the priest's salary, I saw the need for explaining the matter to the majordomo. When I asked him about the priest, the majordomo showed his displeasure, replying: "Dismiss it from your mind; he is no good." "How is that?" I asked. "On one of the holy days," he replied, "while this priest was preaching or announcing the forthcoming holy days of obligation, he made an improper remark, saying that if he wanted to, he could do some harm to someone in this place. Then he warned his hearers not to repeat his remarks to anyone, lest the devil get them." After this happened, the majordomo and some other honorable men went to this priest and begged him in a friendly way to explain what he had meant by his remarks of the day before. The priest replied that it was nothing at all. Then they admonished him more vigorously, insisting on an explanation.

Being thus pressed, the priest . . . [told of a conversation he had overheard between a man and a woman, in which the man had made a blasphemous remark about the Virgin Mary]. They asked the priest to search his memory to recall who it was that said such a thing. The priest swore he did not know who it was; he had only heard that someone had said it, and he did not even remember who told him about it.

This is what the majordomo told me. Nobody else was present nor did I find out any more about it. Since your graces are guardians of the Faith, you might look into this matter, because the people in that area are almost all recent converts from Mohammedanism. People of this type, as your graces know better than I, maintain stubborn doubts about our faith, and about the purity of the virginity of Our Lady. It could be, therefore, that the heretical opinion heard by that priest was held by some of those new converts to the Faith, causing them to lose their souls.

As for himself, Diego said, he had carefully reviewed in his mind everything that had happened since his birth. He wanted to be certain on the final judgment day that Satan would be unable to make any accusations against him. He had undoubtedly been negligent in his speech, repeating blasphemies he had heard from others. Perhaps, too, he had not replied fully to the questions he had been asked under oath. He did not want Satan to have an opportunity to take advantage of any such lapses; therefore he now wished to accuse himself before their graces and to clear his conscience completely.

In Córdoba, for example, Diego now recalled that he had not given a complete list of all his possessions as required by the Inquisitors. The items he failed to list were of minor importance and he does not recall just what they were. However, if their graces would like, he would be happy to make up a complete list now.

Diego then made one of his rare references to his fateful conversation with his accuser Rodrigo Durán:

Among the accusations against me was that when I was speaking one night with a man who was on his way to the New World, I said that Our Lady had not come down from Heaven to the holy church in Toledo, nor had She given Saint Ildefonso a chasuble with which to say mass. I said that this story was not true and that the Church did not so hold. I also maintained I did not know what else in speaking with this man, and I know I spoke badly and wrongly. For this I ask Our Lord for pardon and your graces for penance.

This same man also told me that a later Archbishop of Toledo put on the chasuble despite the objections of the cathedral chapter, and that he blew up in it. I believe I laughed at this story and said it was all a joke, and that the Church did not hold this view. I accuse myself of having had this conversation with this man and of maintaining something else which I do not recall, may God save me.

I said what I did, sirs, without knowing that this story was considered true, nor did I know that it was so commonly talked about. I am therefore especially grieved that I expressed the contrary view. I now state that since devout Christians hold this story to be true, I also accept it as true. . . . I also accuse myself of having said, when talking with this man, that Our Lady had not returned to earth after Her ascension to Heaven. . . . I am grieved at having said this, and I beg God, in His infinite mercy, to forgive me and give me His grace so that I may wisely make this earthly pilgrimage without being tripped up by the devil. I also beg your graces for mercy.

I was also accused of speaking with a youth who was traveling from Illescas to Toledo. He told me that one morning in Guadalupe there appeared a chest with one man inside and another on top. It seems this chest had flown through the air, as God can do anything. I told the youth not to believe this story, and that nobody would go to Hell for not believing it.

On April 21, 1528, I presented a written reply to the accusation of the prosecutor. Although I knew what I had said about the descent of Our Lady [in Toledo], I am not certain if I gave the clear statement demanded by my conscience—I was very disturbed and upset at the time. That is why I now refer to this matter again, because—and may your graces pardon my prolixity—I want my conscience to be clear.

The witnesses mentioned an argument of mine about images. . . . [to the effect that] images are for half-Christians or for people of limited understanding, but not for real Christians or for judicious people. As I recall, I said that images tell stories for the simple people—not that they should not be worshipped in the spirit as symbols of what they represent—for our contemplation and recollection. Through images the simple people can learn what is inaccessible to them in writing. By looking at paintings, retables, or on [painted] walls, at such representations as the Passion of Christ, step by step they [come to] understand those things inaccessible to them in written form. . . .

I beg you, sirs, to disregard the many foolish things I did in the trial. . . . By my unbalanced words I gave many persons occasion to accuse me. . . . Our Lord God allowed this to happen to me so that I might gain more knowledge of the many oppressions and trials of this world. May He be blessed and praised for everything and, sirs, may He illuminate your judgment in this and in everything which you administer in His holy honor.

Toledo: July 22, 1529

On the morning of July 22, seventeen months after he had been denounced by Rodrigo Durán, Diego de Uceda, dressed in the garb of a penitent, was brought out to the *auto de fe* in the public square at Toledo, where the following charges and sentence were read:

We, the Inquisitors against heretical depravity and apostasy in the most noble city and Archbishopric of Toledo, by virtue of authority apostolic and ordinary, have examined a lawsuit pending before us, between the honorable Diego Ortiz de Angulo, prosecutor of this Holy Office, and the accused criminal Diego de Uceda, native of the city of Córdoba, as to the validity of an accusation by the prosecutor, who claims that the accused has committed heresy and apostasy against our Holy Catholic Faith in the following matters and instances:

First, that in speaking of the wicked heresiarch Friar Martin Luther, Diego de Uceda stated and affirmed that Luther spoke well on the subject of confession: that men need confess only to God and not to the priest. When he was reproved and told that the Church teaches the contrary, Diego de Uceda remained in his Lutheran error.

When a certain person said Luther was a terrible heretic, Uceda replied that not everything Luther said was bad, as for example when he said there should be no images at all, that one should worship only God and the Holy Sacrament, that images were for the simple and not for the judicious. He also asked what difference there was between the images in use today and the idols used by the pagans. Being told that the pagans worshipped their images as gods and Christians worshipped them because of the saints in Heaven which they represent, Uceda remained in his error.

A certain person told him that the images of Our Lady of Guadalupe and Montserrat had performed miracles. Uceda said he did not believe a word of it. A certain person told him of the miracle Our Lady had performed in giving to Saint Ildefonso a chasuble with which to say mass, and that a later archbishop who insisted on saying mass with it, had blown up. Diego de Uceda replied that the whole thing was a joke and that there were no miracles; that Our Lady had not come down to earth after her ascension to Heaven.

Diego de Uceda communed with and favored heretics. He committed many heresies and errors against the Faith. . . .

[On the basis of these charges the prosecutor has asked] that we pronounce and declare Diego de Uceda to have been and to be an apostate heretic of our Holy Catholic Faith and Christian religion, and to have incurred sentence of major excommunication, confiscation and loss of all property; that we declare his property to belong to the royal treasury as of the day he committed these crimes against the faith; and that we relax him to the secular arm [i.e., for execution]. . . .

Diego de Uceda [in his defense before us], replied that what he had said about Luther was that it seemed proper to him that the ministers of the Church be poor, as Luther said. If he erred in this regard, he submitted himself to the correction of the Holy Mother Church.

In the matter of confession, Diego de Uceda claimed he had said that confession consists mainly of lamenting and recognizing oneself as a sinner in the soul; that to fulfill the command of the Holy Mother Church one should confess to the priest, weeping over and lamenting his sins and being determined to improve in the future.

As to miracles, Diego de Uceda stated that miracles occur where faith is weak, and that he never denied that Our Lady had power to do everything. Rather he said there was no need to pay so much attention to the things people were saying [about the miracles of Our Lady].

He said he had spoken about Luther and Erasmus and that his hearers might have confused the two. He remembered saying that Luther said there should be no images but that Luther taught many things far worse, and that images served only to demonstrate to the soul what they stood for. As for the story of the chasuble of Saint Ildefonso, it was pious to believe it but it was not an article of the Faith.

Diego de Uceda denied all the other charges. In a statement written in reply to the accusation against him he confessed that he had said he did not believe Our Lady had given the chasuble to Saint Ildefonso, and that such stories were pious, and he asked mercy for having spoken as he did. . . .

[Having duly examined all the evidence in this case], we find that the prosecutor has not completely proven his case. However, evidence of guilt and suspicious behavior has developed from the trial and from the questioning and the confession of Diego de Uceda.

The law allows us to proceed against him with the most serious punishment. However, having mercy on him, we hereby order that now, on the day of this *auto*, he appear as a penitent on the scaffold, barefooted and bareheaded, with a wax candle in his hand; that he here abjure *de vehementi* all crime of heresy, and that he satisfy all the other spiritual and monetary penalties imposed upon him.[1]

Toledo: January 16, 1531

On this date the Inquisitors of the Holy Office of Toledo received two letters from Córdoba:

I, Friar Dionisio de Mesa, of the Order of Saint Dominic, conventual in Saint Paul of Córdoba, hereby state that Diego de

---

[1] The spiritual and monetary penalties were imposed on July 27, five days after Diego's appearance at the *auto de fe*. Diego was required to make seven Saturday pilgrimages to a shrine of his choice, there to recite the *Paternoster* and *Ave Maria* fifteen times each. On any three Fridays he was to fast on a Lenten diet. He was to confess and take communion on the next three major Church festivals (Whitsuntide, Christmas, and Easter), and was required to submit evidence of having done so. He was also fined sixty ducats.

Uceda, native of this city of Córdoba, confessed to me and received from me the Sacrament of the Eucharist at Christmas and Easter of the year 1530. In testimony of this I herewith affix my signature. Dated the last day of Easter, 1530.

Friar Dionisio de Mesa

[P.S.] I also confessed Diego de Uceda on Whitsunday of the same year of 1530, and he took communion also.

* * *

Most reverend sirs: I was ordered by your Holy Office to confess and take communion on the next three major Church festivals, and to send you evidence to this effect. I am sending this evidence by way of the Holy Office of this city. The pressure of work has delayed its arrival until now.

May your graces make up for our defects, and may Our Lord keep and favor your most reverend persons with the prosperity you desire. Córdoba, December 24, 1530.

I kiss the hands of your graces,
Diego de Uceda

Three years after being denounced, Diego de Uceda had been purged of his heresy.

13 *R. Gonsalvius Montanus*
A Sixteenth Century Spanish Prostestant Martyrology

This basically anonymous tract had an enormous impact upon Prostestants during the late sixteenth and early seventeenth centuries, in its several editions and translations from the original Spanish and Latin versions of 1567. Here, the worst fears of the Inquisition, Spain, and Catholicism generally were seemingly confirmed. The author, or authors' limited views on religious toleration are apparent; notice, too, the emphasis, in moral and hortatory terms, on the right of princes with respect to ecclesiastical powers, a typical—and universal—contemporary theme cutting across religious strife. This archetypal Prostestant martyrology contributed much more to prejudicial stereo-

types than all the far numerous processes against Marranos and others, who were not the concern of European Protestants. Indeed, Montanus's sympathies for the converts and non-Christians in this context is rather limited. The translator, of course, is solely concerned with the anti-Protestanism of the story, with its anti-Spanish possibilities; hence he plays on the unpleasant half-Spanish memory of the recent reign of "Bloody Mary," by way of heightening his prefatory remarks, and illuminating the Protestant English wisdom of the Elizabethan regime. In that context he also makes much, successfully no doubt for his readers, of the ongoing Spanish Catholic "inquisitorial" tyranny across the Channel in the Low Countries under Alva's harsh rule. The reader should also note how many subsequent interpretations of the Inquisition may have stemmed from this martyrology, including the attribution of its founding and operations to financial greed.

From the section introducing the work: "The translator to the reader: . . . surely the dangerous practises and most horrible executions of the SPANISH INQUISITION, declared in this book, which now is brought with fire and sword into the Low Countries, the sudden imprisonment of honest men without process of law, the pitiful wandering in exile and poverty of personages sometime rich and wealthy, the wives hanging on their husbands' shoulders, and the poor banished infants on the mothers' breasts, the monstrous racking of men without order of law, the villainous and shameless tormenting of naked women beyond all humanity, their miserable death without pity or mercy, the most reproachful triumphing of the popish Synagogue over Christians. . . , the conquering of subjects as though they were enemies, the unsatiable spoiling of men's goods to fill the [empty]paunches of ambitious idle changelings, the slender quarrels picked against kingdoms and nations, and all this only to hoist up a pield polling (?) priest above all power and au-

SOURCE. R. Gonsalvius Montanus, *A Discovery and Playne Declaration of Sundry Subtill Practices of the Holy Inquisition* (London, 1568), V. Skinner, translator. Selections taken from the translator's preface and the author's preface.

thority that is on earth: these things ought surely much more
to move us to compassion. Being no stage play, but a matter
fit for a Poet to make a Tragedy of hereafter . . . most incredible to them who shall not have seen it . . . [concerning]
our neighbors . . . our friends . . . of the same . . . faith, and
our very brethren in Christ. And if we weep when we see
cruelties set forth in plays, because the like either hath happened
to us . . . or . . . may betide us, then have we not only good
cause in these calamities of our poor brethren to bewail what
is happened to them, but also to fear what will follow upon us.
For if we that not x years since felt but a taste of this iron
whip [Mary Tudor's "bloody" reign, 1553-1558], and since have
enjoyed quietness and leisure to serve God, think ourselves sure
and the storm passed, and that we be but hearers . . . and have
no part in this Tragedy, besides that we are uncharitable in so
lightly esteeming the griefs of others, we do also foolishly and
dangerously abuse ourselves. For who . . . knoweth not . . . of
the holy . . . Conspiracy agreed on by the Pope and his Champions for the execution of the council of Trent, and the general
establishing of this Inquisition? Behold the attempts in Scotland,
the proceedings in France, the executions in Flanders . . . [we
English are next]. . . . If the Devil's holiness, and his lieutenant
general, the Popes . . . were a little moved then, they be now
(doubt ye not) enraged, and . . . in . . . furor . . . , to see
their revenues decay, their monasteries and synagogues defaced,
their villainies detected, their noble champions slain. And therefore you must set before your eyes the DEVIL in person, and
the POPE HIS CHAPLAIN AND CONFESSOR gotten up
into the top of some high mountain, and from thence showing
the kingdoms of the earth to such Princes as will themselves
fall down and worship [them, thereby gaining the world]. Which
. . . is known to be the very Platform and foundation of all
the broils and troubles . . . these men seek no religion. For
how can they . . . that think there is no God? They seek the
honor and wealth of the world. If the Gospel would allow ambition, pleasure, profit, the POPE would have long since been
a Protestant. [There ensues a lengthy and vitriolic assault on the
Papacy] . . . but compare the imprisonments of the persecuted
Protestants, with the restraints on the bridled Papists, their fam-

ine with [the latter's] fatness, their tongues' fettered with iron
torments, with the liberty of railing that our [Catholics, appar-
ently] have and use, seditiously against their prince, and blas-
phemously against God, their most miserable and strange kinds
of deaths, with our men living and liking (?), they shall easily
know the tree and the persons by the fruit. Wherefore (good
reader) having . . . marks of their . . . bloody conspiracy, . . .
the very true cause of all these troubles and wars . . . in Christendom. . . ."

From the author's preface: his description of the Inquisition's
founding, etc.: ". . . a diligent endeavor to remove the infection
that might grow [from] the Jewish and Mohammedan heresies
that daily do arise, besides the revenues of the Exchequer increased hereby, and the sudden and marvelous enriching of
diverse private persons. . . . But . . . by Christ's own saying,
and by natural reason, [the Inquisition is to be judged by its
fruits] . . . [thus I shall evaluate it] . . . no man will doubt but
that this tree . . . deserves to be hewed down, if there be
sufficient proof that it buds forth such pestilent blossoms . . . it
were a dangerous . . . matter, if we heretics that detest the
Inquisition as a sharp and just plague of God, . . . should have
any credit given us herein [for demonstrating the Inquisition's
iniquity] . . . I have thought it . . . worth . . . the travail, to
show [in] the briefest and most certain way, whereby the truth
thereof might without any great trouble be understood. [For-
mal procedures for investigating and judging the Inquisition
are set forth]. . . . For . . . which purposes those that . . . are,
or have been . . . in the Inquisitors' prisons, were first to be
sent for and examined but unbridled . . . [describes the pur-
ported methods the inquisitors used to achieve their victims'
silence, even after prison and noncapital punishment]. . . .

. . . it is . . . greatly pertinent to our purpose, to show how
we came to the knowledge [of the Inquisition] . . . all this is
true . . . [notes he will pass over the matter of the "king's treasury" in this regard, so as to avoid being accused of "envy," but
then touches on the confiscated properties of the 'many thousands' of Jews, Moors, and heretics involved]. . . .

. . . [With the Catholic Kings' reign] . . . considering that those
people [conversos] were but only Christians by name and for

fashion's sake, submitting themselves for fear and awe, and for
. . . their riches rather than any love or zeal which they bore
to Christianity, desired to make provision . . . for their better
instruction. A godly purpose surely . . . if evil counsellors had
not maliciously perverted their good intents . . . [the Dominicans who] became a proud and ambitious sect . . . kings were
content to be ordered and directed by them . . . whereas they
should have provided godly instructors . . . to win and allure
the counterfeit Christians . . . by charity and gentleness . . .
[instead] they erected a new . . . Inquisition, wherein the poor
wretches . . . should be robbed and spoiled of all their goods
and possessions, and either put to cruel death, or suffer most
intolerable torments by whip or otherwise, leading the rest of
their lives in perpetual obloquy and ignominy, and sustaining
extreme poverty. . . . Neither was this executed only upon
such, as had most shamefully blasphemed Christ but [for] the
least and most trifling ceremony of the *Jewish* or *Moorish*
law, or the smallest error in Christian religion [never giving true
religious instruction] . . . Sixtus IV . . . Pope of Rome, . . .
add[ed] his confirmation, so that at length [the Inquisition] became of such force . . . that were it not for that the hugeness
thereof is such, that it is not able to sustain itself, being a thing
so burdensome to the world . . . a man might very well think
it to be impregnable . . . [the tribunal is lambasted at length for
its cruelty]. . . . As the *Dominicans* were [its] first authors . . .
they obtained the execution of this tyranny under the pretence
of teaching the true Christian faith, whereof they had of long
. . . been accepted the patrons. But afterwards by means of
their insatiable covetousness and ambition (for the which two
vices they are already discredited among the common people)
as also for their cruelty and tyranny . . . they became so intolerable, that the Princes themselves . . . were . . . forced to dis-
place them, pretending diverse reasonable causes and allegations.
. . . [This seems a kind of wish fulfillment on the writer's part.
Ed.]

. . . we may thank these wicked counsellors and none other
for the Inquisition at this day, most devlishly perverting the
godly purposes of the Princes . . . [why] else . . . should [they]
erect a new kind of *Consistory* so rare and strange . . . , which

is not set up to inform the ignorant, or to convince the obstinate, and bring them to . . . true religion, either by . . . learning, or by charitable dealing the only means that Christ [used and approved], but to compel them by force and might, by rigor and extremity . . . by *Racks and Torments, Chains, Halters, Barnacles, Sanbenitos* by *Fire* and by *Faggots* . . . think ye, that all these things were devised rather to lay new taxes and impositions upon the people . . . then for the furtherance of religion . . .

This Inquisition you will say was not brought in [for religious instructional purposes], but only that heresy . . . might be abolished: . . . so much we yield . . . [there follows a lengthy description of the presumed stagnant, corrupt character of Spanish Catholicism generally]. . . . And the court of Inquisition being erected . . . for reformation of errors [in contrast to popular teaching of the faith, however poorly executed . . . such a separation of functions should not have been permitted] that the authority committed to the bishops by the Holy Scriptures of God, should . . . be taken from them: neither should . . . any other fire and sword . . . root out heresies, but only the sword of God's word. . . . For surely a true and justifying faith cannot be forced . . . no more than can heresy be destroyed by the heretic's death. . . . For thereby faith is not only engendered, but increased . . . marvelously . . . [a man's religion should be examined in a scriptural light with excommunication the last resort in face of obstinacy; profiting from heresy by confiscation, etc., is unchristian. The author relies chiefly upon St. Paul here.]. . . . As concerning the putting of heretics to death, it is like . . . a Physician . . . [intending] to rid the patient of his disease, should for the nonce rid him also of his life . . . by taking away his life, they cut him off from all those means and possibilities whereby he might attain . . . salvation . . . God's judgments are deep and imcomprehensible. . . . But it is to be feared . . . [that one accused or condemned by the Inquisition] will . . . infect others. True it is and for that consideration, both Christ and his Apostles commandeth us to eschew him, and cut him off from the body of the church. But . . . they would . . . proceed farther . . . [to] punish such obstinate persons more severely, were not the ordinary magistrate sufficient to execute the same . . . [an analysis of secular as against inquisitorial-Dominican judgment in such matters follows, defending the former] . . . [canonists and clergy are broadly described as] such ignorant men . . . admitted to determine matters of Religion, as have no . . . knowledge in the Holy Scriptures . . . they must needs turn sweet into sour, and sour into sweet: call light darkness, and darkness light . . . in professing themselves . . . Patrons of faith, root out all faith, and maintain monstrous errors: flee the children of God, and cherish the children of the Devil: kill the servants of Christ, foster, maintain, and increase the servants of Antichrist. . . ."

CONCLUSION

Established to protect Spanish Catholicism from an apparently grave internal menace, the Inquisition purified the national faith with great success in a narrowly-construed and rigidly orthodox manner. To assist it in this primary task, successive governments expelled and forcibly converted Jews and Moslems, thereby increasing in several comprehensive strokes the numbers of the always-suspect New Christians. Those forms of Catholicism itself which seemingly failed to hue to the faith as inquisitorially defined—and often popularly understood—also fell within the Holy Office's increasingly omniscient purview. The rise of international and institutional forms of Protestantism, on Spain's own northern border in the case of French Calvinism, led to the broadening of the Inquisition's scope and methods, as indicated by its growing control of book censorship during the sixteenth century. Throughout, it received broad popular, national support, from prince to peasant.

The price paid for this method of preserving a restrictively interpreted, quasi-racist religion, and what was understood to be the prerequisite for continued national unity, was, in conjunction with other aspects of Spanish life, a general shrinking of national horizons in their intellectual, cultural, and religious expressions. As Márquez Villanueva eloquently observes in the selection from his essay, the tragic profundity of the conversos' situation was that many sought to be more perfect Catholics in a society much less Christian than it claimed and sought to be; the original taint (or sin) of blood could never be effaced, and those who, like the Jesuits in the beginning, tried to combat this fought a losing battle and even they succumbed, in Spain, to prevailing attitudes. Christian charity and piety in perhaps the most catholic sense went by the boards.

Such assessments must, of course, be qualified with the equally valid observation that this era of Spanish history, the "Golden

Age" of Cervantes, Lope de Vega, Las Casas, and innumerable others, ran parallel with the heyday of the Holy Office, as well as Spanish political and military greatness. Still, there is little doubt but that the Inquisition helped to undermine, in the widest sense, the society which produced these great figures and achievements. Furthermore, it lingered on in an often successful holding operation against new, frequently foreign developments, long past the years when that Golden Age had faded into memory, and when Spain required new attitudes in order to progress beyond that too nostalgically viewed era.

Thus the Inquisition, abetted by contemporary Reformation martyrologists, anticlerical Spaniards of a later day, and often patronizing foreigners of the modern period, became a significant part of the myth of Spain as the land of the "Black Legend," that half-African province of Europe. The subtle shadings of the story, increasingly freed from bias of varying kinds, have begun to be examined only recently. As I have noted often, Spaniards as well as outsiders are still grappling with the Inquisition's full meaning for the understanding of the Spanish experience.

Perhaps the Inquisition's most enduringly retrograde accomplishment is best summed up by the scrupulously fair words of John Elliott from another section of his *Imperial Spain*: "Spain . . . alone was a multi-racial society . . . the insistence on the most rigorous orthodoxy represented a desperate attempt to deal with a problem of unparalleled complexity; and it is hardly surprising if religious uniformity appeared as the sole guarantee of national survival. . . . The price paid for the adoption of this policy proved . . . to be very high, but it is understandable enough that to contemporaries the cost of *not* adopting it should have seemed even higher . . . [by the end of the seventeenth century Spanish] society had lost the strength that comes from dissent, and . . . lacked the vision and strength of character to break with a past that could no longer serve as a reliable guide to the future. . . . At a time when the face of Europe was altering more rapidly than ever before, the country that had once been its leading power proved to be lacking the essential ingredient . . . the willingness to change" (pp. 376-78).

The lesson for our own time is obvious enough.

BIBLIOGRAPHICAL ESSAY

The following assumes those already cited fully in the readings.

Some general studies that have useful pages on the Inquisition and related affairs are Roger B. Merriman, *The Rise of The Spanish Empire* (New York, 1918–1932; reprinted, 1962), whose four volumes provide a very detailed account of political and institutional developments from the middle ages to the reign of Philip II; Richard Herr's *The Eighteenth Century Revolution in Spain* (Princeton, N.J., 1958) carries the story to the Inquisition's confrontation with the impact of the Enlightment in Spain; and Raymond Carr's monumental *Modern Spain, 1808–1939* (Oxford University Press, 1966) has some succinctly done background discussion for this and other topics. My own brief review article, "Pablo de Olavide and Disunity in the Spanish Enlightenment," *Historical Journal,* VIII (1965), pp. 112–116 touches on the Inquisition's relationship to some leading Spanish reformers of that period. Henry Kamen's uneven *Rise of Toleration** (New York, 1967) discussed this subject mainly in the sixteenth century for Europe as a whole; much more provocative on religious heterodoxy in the middle ages and early modern period generally is Norman Cohn's *Pursuit of the Millenium** (New York, 1961).

Cohn has just published *Warrant for Genocide* (London, 1967), which traces European Christianity's inherent anti-Semitism up through the Nazi holocaust, but with much attention devoted to the periods relevant to the Spanish Inquisition. Several general histories of the Jews treat this area but, as noted in the introduction, I have found Y.F. Baer's *A History of the Jews in Christian Spain*, Vol. II (Philadelphia, Pa., 1966) most helpful. The Américo Castro tome often referred to, and also his only work available in English, is *The Structure of Spanish History*, E.L. King, translator (Princeton, N.J., 1954). Two

---

* The asterick indicates paper editions.

other very germane essays from the collection honoring Castro's 80th year, cited in the Márquez Villanueva selection, are "Historical Research on Spanish Conversos in the Last 15 Years" by Antonio Dominguez Ortiz, one of Spain's most distinguished scholars, and "Américo Castro, Luis de Léon, and the Inner Tensions of Spain's Golden Age" by Manuel Durán; these are on pp. 317–333 and 83–90, respectively.

For the interrelationship among Erasmism, Illuminism, and Protestantism, real and imagined, I have summarized my article, "Reform and Counterreform: The Case of the Spanish Heretics," in a memorial volume of essays dedicated to E.H. Harbison, the late Reformation historian of Princeton University, *Action and Conviction in Early Modern Europe* (Princeton, 1969), pp. 154–68. John E. Longhurst's numerous articles and monographs, besides the Uceda one, are very important in this area. The standard work on Spanish Erasmism is Marcel Bataillon's *Erasme et L'Espagne* (Paris, 1937), translated and revised in a two-volume Spanish version in 1950. Menéndez y Pelayo's famous study alluded to is the multivolume and often reissued *Historia de los heterodoxos españoles*. Albert A. Sicroff's outstanding monograph on the purity of blood statutes must be noted: *Les Controverses des Statutes de "Pureté de Sang" en Espange du XV° au XVII° Siècle* (Paris, 1960). One hopes for English translations of the Bataillon and Sicroff works, especially since Professor Sicroff is on the faculty of an American university.

On witchcraft see the ensuing book of readings on the subject in this series by E. William Monter of Northwestern University; *The World of Witches* (Chicago, 1964), by Julio Caro Baroja which is devoted to the phenomenon in Spain; and the fascinating two-part article by H.R. Trevor-Roper, "The Witchcraft Craze," *Encounter Magazine*, May-June, 1967, which has just been reprinted in a new collection of essays by this noted British historian. The best starting point on the Moriscos are the relevant chapters in Lea's study, cited in Part One. The Elliott and Lynch books are rich in bibliographical suggestions in all areas of early modern Spanish history.

Several broader helpful general works are the new and well-executed broad analysis, *The Fifteenth Century: The Prospect of Europe** (New York, 1968) by Margaret Aston, providing illuminating discussion of religious discontent and impulses toward reform, as well as other matters. Harold J. Grimm's *The Reformation Era* (New

York, 1954, 1966) remains the standard English-language compendium on the subject, with some data on Spain and Spanish Catholicism, but two more recent analytical, selective discussions, *Reformation Europe, 1517–1559** (New York, 1966) by G.R. Elton and *Reformation and Society in Sixteenth Century Europe** (New York, 1966) by A.G. Dickens are much more penetrating and excitingly put together. Just out are *Europe Divided, 1559–98** (New York, 1969) by J.H. Elliott, *Europe in the 16th Century* by H.L. Koenigsberger and Geo. Mosse (New York, 1969), and *The Counterreformation* (New York, 1969) by A.G. Dickens, all of which, with the 2 items just cited, truly update 16th century general historiography. Useful materials on areas of Spanish religion are scattered throughout George H. Williams' massive synthesis, *The Radical Reformation* (Philadelphia, Pa., 1962).